ECONOMIC ISSUES
in Immigration

Economic Issues in Immigration

An exploration of the liberal approach
to public policy on immigration

CHARLES WILSON   DAVID COLLARD

W. H. HUTT   E. J. MISHAN

SUDHA SHENOY   GRAHAM HALLETT

With an Introduction by

SIR ARNOLD PLANT

Published by

The Institute of Economic Affairs
1970

First published 1970 by

The Institute of Economic Affairs

© 1970

SBN 255 35982-9

331.62042   WILS

46099

 PRINTED BY Unwin Brothers Limited
THE GRESHAM PRESS OLD WOKING SURREY ENGLAND

Produced by 'Uneoprint'

A member of the Staples Printing Group   (UO8017)

Contents

Introduction

by *SIR ARNOLD PLANT*

Historians of Britain's agricultural, industrial, commercial and
financial development since medieval times have familiarised us all
with the notable contribution made to this country's economic growth
and strength by alien immigrants from Europe. On the whole, our
governments encouraged them to come, protected their settlements
from the natural hostility of local inhabitants and were content to
tax rather than expropriate the financiers among them, with the re-
grettable and notorious exceptions of some impecunious monarchs.
Such antagonism as was shown by the British people to foreign settlers was generally no different in kind from that aroused by internal
migrants from other parts of the country, nor indeed from that habitually displayed against long-settled inhabitants of adjacent hamlets
and towns. In this century the revolution in road and rail transport
has shown up these local prejudices for the nonsense they always
were, but some of us are old enough to remember how large a part
they played in enlivening local gossip in country homes and inns.

As the London-born son of a mother brought up in the Peak of Derby-
shire, I spent my early holidays when a small boy with working-class
grandparents and uncles and aunts. Coming as I did from Shoreditch,
where the bakers and barbers and tailors were mostly German
immigrants, the timber merchants and cabinet-makers from Russia
and Eastern Europe, and so on, I was fascinated to be told how gorm-
less were the contemptible dwellers in near-by villages and towns.
A son or daughter who married and brought home one of these 'furriners' was chided for lowering the purity and sturdiness of the local
stock. My grandmother explained to me that my mother's lamentable
emigration to London was the disastrous consequence of her marry-
ing a furriner drawn from an ancient North Staffordshire family
living twelve miles away. Until she died full of years, my grandmother
never did, nor aspired to, see the sea, and resolutely refused to visit
us in London. The immigrants from Europe differed only in that their
talk on first arrival was even less intelligible than the dialects of
local furriners, and their manners suspiciously better, almost ingra-
tiating. One's children were not encouraged to develop too intimate
a relationship with theirs. Inter-racial marriages 'bring out the worst
of both sides, tha' knows'.

After the accession of William and Mary to the throne, the arrival of
a new stream of immigrants from Holland aroused the usual reactions.
That well-travelled publicist, Daniel Defoe, a loyal supporter of King
William, published in 1701 his satire *The True-born Englishman* which,

by the wit and outspokenness of its rhyming couplets and the rapidity
with which over 20 editions were sold in two years, became the most
popular piece published in King William's reign. Thereafter, no
literate person in the country, indeed no one who was not too stupid to
grasp the purport of what was read out to him, would wisely profess to
be 'true born' or, if he did, claim that there was any virtue apart from
dubious rarity attaching to his peculiarity. In a preface, Defoe remarked that

> 'if I were to write a reverse to the satire, I would examine all
> the nations of Europe, and prove that those nations which are
> most mixed are the best, and have least of barbarism and brut-
> ality among them; and abundance of reasons might be given for
> it'.

I must resist the strong temptation to quote here any of the 1,100 or
so lines of satire by which Defoe shatters the myth of the true-born
Englishman. It is clear (though not explicitly) from Professor
Charles Wilson's admirable contribution 'The Immigrant in English
History', printed first in this collection of six essays, that he knows
his Defoe, and I am grateful in part for his essay because it has
prompted me to read the satire once again.

It so happens that while I was engaged in reading these essays and
writing this Introduction, there came into my hands the recently
published lectures delivered in the University of Ghana in 1968 by
Professor Sir W. Arthur Lewis, my old friend and former academic
colleague, under the title *Some Aspects of Economic Development*
(distributed in this country by Allen and Unwin). This is the sixth
series of Aggrey-Fraser-Guggisberg Memorial Lectures first insti-
tuted in 1957 with funds provided by the Government of Ghana to
commemorate these three founders of Achimota College. Professor
Lewis (now at Princeton) is a native of the West Indian island of
St. Lucia, who in the course of his varied and distinguished academic
career has served as Principal and Vice-Chancellor of the University of the West Indies. In the third of his five lectures, on 'Development Planning', he discusses the problems created by the migration
of foreigners, members of traditionally trading communities, into
tropical Asian and African areas which had hitherto functioned only
as subsistence societies. In this lecture Professor Lewis draws upon
his careful study and sympathetic understanding of the history of immigration policy in Britain to formulate proposals for the improvement of immigration policy (such as it is) in the newly-independent
tropical countries. I shall therefore summarise his argument
here partly quoting (as I am sure he would approve and prefer) his
own well-chosen words.

> 'The Chinese swarmed over South-east Asia; the Indian traders
> opened up Burma, and then East Africa; Syrians and Lebanese
> moved into West Africa. And at a later stage, the Ibos of Southern

Nigeria, having learned the techniques of trading, moved north into the Muslim states in large numbers. There is no doubt that these traders performed a service without which rapid development would not have been possible... It is beyond question that they raised the economic level of the peasants as well as themselves by what they did.'

Why were they so successful?

'Mainly because their culture is different from that of farmers in subsistence societies. They are willing to work 18 hours a day for six days a week... In addition they have the virtues one finds in any immigrant group. Immigrants know that their success depends on their own efforts, and therefore they live by higher standards of effort and personal responsibility than people who are living in their own country. It follows also that such groups are clannish. When they have a job they hire one of their own, because they know from bitter experience that the natives among whom they live do not live by the code which success in business requires... It is not race that gives Indians or Chinese or Arabs or Ibos their superior accomplishment when they live in subsistence societies. The difference is wholly in the culture of immigration. Whatever the cause, the result in the second half of the twentieth century is explosive. As the indigenous populations have tried to enter business they have found themselves largely unable to compete, because they do not understand what business takes. The method of learning, which would be to apprentice their sons in other people's businesses, is closed to them... So antagonisms have got fiercer until they have erupted in violent and disgusting outbursts. The story began in Burma, where shortly after independence all the Indians were driven out... Then the position of the Chinese in Thailand and in Indonesia began to be threatened: a massacre of these people one of these days is not yet out of the question. Here [in Africa] the Northerners killed 20,000 Ibos in September 1966 and drove out a million from their homes. The Indians in East Africa are clearly doomed, the only question being how many will be killed before they are all driven out. Genocide is the favourite crime of our century... Different races cannot live at peace within the same borders unless there is absolute economic equality between them. Racial differences bring enough trouble without their being identified also with economic conflicts.'

What can be done? Professor Lewis continues:

'For examples we can go quite far back in British history. In the year 1484, when large numbers of silk weavers were flooding England from France, they were welcomed by Richard III because they were bringing in a new industry. But in order to prevent them from developing into a separate clan, and in order to force them to teach their trade to English youngsters, he passed an Act forbidding a foreigner to take any other foreigner as an apprentice except his son. Henry VIII faced a similar and equally welcome influx of Protestant refugees from Holland some 40 years later. He strengthened the Act in 1523 by forbidding aliens to have any alien apprentices at all. The new skills were therefore acquired by Englishmen within a generation. This is what the Northerners should have done to the Ibos instead of murdering them. A law prohibiting non-Northerners from employing other non-Northerners, coupled with a massive educational programme for Northerners, would have solved the problem within a generation'.

Professor Lewis's confident optimism concerning the efficacy of his plan to follow particular British precedents bears witness to his sense of the desperately urgent need to counter the threat of violence and mass genocide by enforcing absolute economic equality of opportunity between the indigenous and immigrant races. The parallel he draws between 15th and 16th century Britain and tropical countries in the 20th century is illuminating and valuable, and commands our utmost respect, provided only that the defencelessness of the immigrants is closely similar in the two cases. In Britain 500 years ago they were the victims of persecution in their countries of origin, and Britain was their only haven offering a reasonable hope of economic and personal security for themselves and their families. Onerous conditions could therefore be imposed upon their freedom as aliens in Britain to develop their crafts and small businesses in the most efficient and productive way without depriving the country of all the immediate benefits accruing from their special skills, enterprise and industrious habits. Professor Lewis's parallel is therefore most apt in relation to the unhappy plight of Indians today facing ruin, if not worse, in the new independent states of East Africa, and of the Indians and Chinese in parts of South-East Asia. Is it, however, equally applicable to the immigrant Ibos in the Northern states of West Africa? Had they no alternative in Southern Nigeria but to emigrate to the North? Did they migrate to escape oppression or intolerable restrictions in the South on their rights to develop their trading businesses in the way they considered most effective and profitable? Apparently not; did they not go North in the belief that their profits would be higher there? If that is so, how successful would Northern attempts be to impose by legislation profit-reducing restrictions on their freedom to conduct their businesses as they thought best for themselves? Could they not transfer their trading businesses back to the South? Or does Professor Lewis envisage the imposition of restrictions on Ibo traders throughout the whole Federal region, relying on other States also to deny themselves the full economic benefits which they would gain from Ibo traders' efficiency and liking for long hours and hard work?

One device for attracting suitable and willing immigrants to speed up economic growth is the indentured labour contract for a fixed period, with or without compulsory or voluntary repatriation on the completion of the contract. On reflection it is strange that the adoption of this system in the former British Empire has aroused so much animosity in this country among self-styled 'humanitarians'. Something very akin operated on our internal labour market for some centuries, since the days of the medieval wage-fairs. A similar system has long been regarded as a sensible and humane method of recruitment of nationals into our armed Services (and indeed of aliens into the Foreign legions)—a vast improvement, say, on the former Naval press gang. As the authors of the 1948 Report by PEP on *Population Policy in Great Britain* opined, provided that the contract is freely entered into, 'there is no injustice in recruiting immigrants, under contract, for a particular industry and in making their stay in the country conditional on remaining with it for a stated period'. They thought that the admission of immigrants to work in particular industries was at that time 'temporarily desirable'.

South African mining companies have habitually recruited African workers for the diamond and gold mines on the same basis. During the last century the South African colonial governments also recruited alien immigrants from overseas under formal indentured labour contracts: first Indians and later Chinese. The Indian immigrants served their indenture terms mainly on the coastal plantations of Natal, and few of them elected to be repatriated. They took up other occupations or became traders. Some migrated to Cape Colony and the Transvaal. In 1904 there were 100,000 Indians in Natal against 97,000 Europeans. The circumstances in which Chinese indentured immigrants entered the Transvaal at the beginning of the 20th century were special. The South African War had dislocated the arrangements of the gold mining companies for recruiting African labour, and the general economic recovery of the colony depended upon the rapid re-expansion of gold production. The Chinese immigrants were to stand in for African labour, doing only the same work. In January 1904 the Conservative Colonial Secretary in Britain gave his assent to an Ordinance of the Transvaal Legislative Council authorising the importation of indentured labour. The first Chinese arrived in July 1904, and by January 1907 the number employed was 53,856. The gap was partially filled by this 'pump-priming', and the impetus to spectacular economic expansion throughout the Transvaal was thereby restored. Humanitarian opposition in Britain to this so-called 'Chinese Slavery' played a leading part in securing the victory of the Liberal party at the British general election of January 1906. The Liberal Government prohibited the issue of further immigration licences, and insisted upon the termination of the Ordinance one year after the first meeting of the new self-governing Transvaal Legislature in 1907. It was decided that the Chinese labourers should be repatriated as their contracts expired. Australia and New Zealand, having participated in the South African war, had no compunction in making their indignant voices heard on the very idea of permitting Asiatic immigration into any British Dominion in the Southern Hemisphere.

In looking back at the early history of permanent white settlement in South Africa, it is worth recalling that at the very outset in 1652 the first Commandant of the Dutch station in Table Bay, where Cape Town now stands, would have promptly arranged the immigration of free Chinese colonists, if he had been allowed to have his way, to assist in establishing an economically viable foothold in the continent. Had his masters been the new Confederation Government of the Seven Dutch Republics, and had their desire been to establish a colony, he might have got his way. Jan van Riebeeck landed with 181 men, many of them sick. After a fortnight's quick survey of the terrain around the slopes of Table Mountain he recorded that he found everywhere

> 'the finest flat clay ground and other beautiful, broad, fertile soil
> —as fine as one could find anywhere in the world. [He had travel-
> led extensively, and served for years in the Far East.] With the
> small number of men we have, however, not one hundredth part
> of it could be ploughed or cultivated. It would, therefore, be
> suitable if some industrious Chinese were to come here for that
> purpose with all kinds of seeds and plants, for much better fruits
> could be expected here than could be hoped for at Ilha Formosa,
> as the soil is richer, and there are several marshy places'.

Alas, Jan van Riebeeck was not the executive representative of a colonising Republic, but a Commandant responsible to the Governor-General and Council of a monopolistic Dutch East India Company with headquarters in Batavia, intent on establishing at the Cape of Good Hope no more than a refreshment station for ships passing between Holland and the Far East. The last thing the company wanted was the competition of free immigrants in or round about its station, spoiling the lucrative market of provisioning alien ships putting in for supplies. Riebeeck was firmly advised to say no more about the usefulness of free families 'raising crops and cattle and for making butter and cheese', and thenceforward he 'kept mum', making do with his original 181 men, and the services of sick members of ships' companies put ashore for convalescence at the refreshment station. This was 250 years before the introduction of Chinese indentured labourers into the Transvaal was to cause such an outcry in British politics.

Indentured labour contracts have continually run into difficulties concerning repatriation. The terms of contract normally require the approval of the government of the country from which the immigrants are drawn, as well as of the host country. As between India and Natal, the Indian government refused to sanction contracts which made the subsequent repatriation of the immigrants compulsory. The longer the sojourn abroad, the bigger the political and administrative problems of re-absorption, especially with expanding family units. Even given the utmost goodwill on both sides and a sincere determination to give sympathetic consideration to the aspirations of the immigrant and his family, agreement between the parties could prove impossible. How much bigger the problems are after the lapse of several generations!

It is not reasonable for an African government today to regard the descendants of immigrants of long ago as 'aliens' who must be deported or suffer harsh personal and economic discrimination, if not worse. This is the desperate situation to which Sir Arthur Lewis has called attention in the lecture from which I have quoted. Nor, in my view, can it be reasonable for anyone to contend that the present government of a country like India, concerned with its own population problem, is under any special moral obligation to try to create a new home for the vastly larger number of descendants of the Indian emigrants who crossed the sea to Africa perhaps a century ago.

There is another aspect of schemes for immigration under contract to which I wish to refer. I have already called attention to the views of the authors of the 1948 PEP Report on Population Policy. The factual account which that Report gave of the governmental machinery for immigration control was very enlightening to a non-specialist reader such as myself. I cannot recall seeing since then any detailed comprehensive study of the evolution of this control machinery, the criteria to which governments have appealed in operating it, and the economic implications of the decisions taken.

As I understand the position, immigration control in Britain stems from the Aliens Act of 1905, as amended by the Aliens Restriction Acts of 1914 and 1919. Under this legislation, the Aliens Order of 1920 was issued, and this Order still provides the basis of control. To quote some passages from the PEP Report of 1948:

> 'The Home Secretary can prohibit the entry of any non-British national and also has power to order the deportation of aliens on certain grounds, though as to the admission of immigrants wishing to take up employment he is guided by the Minister of Labour'.

Then follows what is to me a tendentious passage:

> 'In so far as immigrants are permanently satisfied with lower standards... they constitute a threat to the interests of the British working class... The sweated industries which developed in Britain half a century ago depended largely on the exploitation of immigrants...'

The Report then went on to explain that

> 'As a rule it is the Government's policy to place foreign labour only in jobs where suitable British labour is not available. The Government schemes are supported by the Minister of Labour's

> Joint Consultative Committee, on which the Trades Union Congress is represented...'

The Report does, however, record that

> 'The Economic Survey for 1947 declared that 'The old arguments against foreign labour are no longer valid'. The price of safe-guarding the interests of British labour in this way has been a much slower rate of absorption of foreign workers than might have been hoped, particularly in the case of mining'.

I find this account of the situation in 1948 very disturbing. To me, it is altogether too reminiscent of South African controls, as I knew them years ago, of immigration and migration in the supposed interests of civilised white labour. How have the British machinery and govern-mental attitudes and policy concerning immigration control changed over the last 22 years? As regards the factual position, I know that the British Nationality Act of 1948 introduced a new term 'citizenship', so that British subjects of the United Kingdom and Colonies became also citizens; and that the Act also specified the conditions under which application could be made for a Certificate of Naturalisation. I am aware also that it sets out the circumstances in which naturalised persons can be deprived of 'citizenship'. It has not entirely escaped my notice that since 1958, with the attainment of independence by former Colonies and dependencies, a series of Acts each relating to a specific former dependency contain special provisions with regard to loss of UK citizenship concerning that State.

What effect has all this had on immigration into the United Kingdom? The six learned contributors whose essays are presented in this collection have provided a formidable and rich meal for our enjoy-ment. Readers with digestions as weak as mine may find some of the ingredients difficult to assimilate. In such circumstances one hesitates to ask, like Oliver Twist, for more: but I for one would welcome another study. I think that many of us need to have, as soon as may be, an account both factual and analytical, both comprehen-sive and in detail, of the evolution of government legislation, pro-cedures, attitudes and policies concerning the immigration of foreign workers into the United Kingdom from 1945 to the present day. Is there a volunteer?

I have been much enlightened by my study of these essays, and I warmly commend them to others.

April 1970   *Arnold Plant*

1. THE IMMIGRANT IN ENGLISH HISTORY

CHARLES WILSON
Professor of Modern History,
Jesus College, Cambridge

THE AUTHOR

Charles Wilson was born in 1914 and educated at De Aston Grammar School, Lincolnshire, and Jesus College, Cambridge, of which he has been a Fellow since 1938 (and Bursar 1945-55). He has been Professor of Modern History in the University of Cambridge since 1963 (previously Reader in Modern Economic History). 1968-69 Ford Lecturer in English History, Oxford University. Litt.D., University of Groningen, 1964. Corresponding Fellow, Royal Danish Academy of Arts and Sciences (1970).

Professor Wilson was joint editor of the *Economic History Review*, 1960-67. His publications include *Anglo-Dutch Commerce and Finance in the 18th Century* (1940); *Holland and Britain* (1945); *History of Unilever* (1954); *Profit and Power* (1957); *England's Apprenticeship 1603-1763* (1965); *Economic History and the Historian* (1969); and numerous articles in learned journals.

—Saxon, or Norman or Dane are we—

sang Tennyson triumphantly. His list is noticeably brief and Nordic
and there is no mention of Briton or Celt: whether this is due to the
exigencies of rhyme and metre or to a partiality (shared by most
Victorian liberals) for the Northern and Teutonic cultures it is difficult now to say. But he could have lengthened his list by adding
Jews (Sephardic and Ashkenazic), Italians, Flemings, Walloons, Dutch,
French Huguenots, Germans, not forgetting Irish and Scots (both regarded by many Englishmen down to the Victorian age as a kind of
foreigner). The richness and variety of English life and culture owes
a great deal to immigration and immigrants. Does their experience
of England or England's experience of them suggest any lesson for
the present?

I. EARLY INTOLERANCE

English society in 1066, with its continuing gulf between Anglo-Saxon
and Norman French, might not be homogeneous (the myth of 'the
Norman yoke' was successfully revived in the 17th century),[1] but it
was Christian—at any rate officially. The one exception, numerically
not large but important, to this generalisation was the Jews. Their
history forms a disagreeable chapter in English medieval history.
The Jews were alien by origins, race, religion and habit. According
to tradition they arrived from Rouen at the invitation of William the
Conqueror, and having come under the royal protection they remained
under it, for good and ill. Throughout the 11th and 12th centuries im-
poverished kings and barons looked to them for large loans, secured
on property. As a counterweight to the financial hold the Jews had
over the rulers, the rulers created an Exchequer of the Jews; and if
the lenders exploited, they were more than counter-exploited by the
borrowers. In the 13th century their situation steadily deteriorated
until, in 1290, sharply prompted by the Pope, Edward I expelled all
Jews from England.

For all that a few of them were wealthy, their situation in England—as
in many other countries—was never anything but precarious. In the
towns where Jewish colonies existed—London, York, Lincoln, Durham,

---

[1] Christopher Hill, *Puritanism and Revolution,* Secker and Warburg,
     1958.

Norwich, Bury St. Edmunds, Stamford—they were the object of popular attack: a violent outbreak in 1189 suggested the possibility of whole-sale massacre. Legends like that of Little St. Hugh of Lincoln sprang up to provide popular excuse for brutal victimisation. St. Hugh was a Christian child alleged to have been lured into a Jewish house at Lincoln, cruelly murdered and flung into a well. The story lingered on till Chaucer's *Prioress's Tale*. It was a variant of a ritual murder legend widely spread over all Europe which survived into the 20th century as a pretext for pogroms in Russia.

Anti-semitism

What was the basis of English medieval anti-semitism? Not—as in later ages—fear of their competition for employment or trade, for the simple reason that they were virtually excluded from most occupations except money-lending. This did not exclude the economic motive entirely. Jealousy of relatively well-to-do Jews like Aaron of Lincoln (whose house still exists on the Steep Hill below the Cathedral) was probably a factor. Indeed, the hatred of debtor for creditor probably played a part everywhere down to the villages where the village Jew did a little pawn-broking with tradesman or peasant. Hatred born of the fear of strangers and strangeness was the most general, popular cause of anti-semitism. But, officially, and to a great extent genuinely, the root of the trouble was religious. This is indicated by the establishment of 'Houses for Converted Jews' founded from the time of Henry II onwards in London, Oxford and Bristol. These show that at any rate Jewish race was not the admit-ted cause of discrimination, because presumably the convert became entitled to full citizenship.

About 16,000 Jews left England under Edward's expulsion order. This was probably a peak figure if we assume that the Jewish popula-tion presumably kept pace with the demographic growth that char-acterised the 12th and 13th centuries generally. Assuming a total population of $1\frac{1}{2}$ to 2 million, the Jews can have represented barely 1 per cent of the whole, though they would of course be a somewhat larger proportion in the bigger towns.

Few English Jews survived the expulsion. One family which claims to have done so is that of the late A. M. Samuel, MP, Lord Mayor of Norwich (1912-13), first Lord Mancroft, and his son, the present Lord Mancroft, whose title is taken from the Norwich parish where their ancestors may have lived.

Anti-Italianism

The necessary successors in office to the Jews in high finance were the Italians. It is more difficult to obtain any clear idea of the number of them permanently resident in England. It was probably not large

outside London and Southampton, where a permanent colony was
needed to manage the business arising out of visits of the Venetian
galleys on their way up the Channel. Not being excluded by religion
from normal trading business, the Italians had a far wider and more
varied range of activities than the Jews. The big men, like the Flor-
entine Bardi, Peruzzi and Frescobaldi, were really royal bankers and
creditors, now discharging the traditional occupation of the great
'Court Jews' by bridging the gap between the income and expenditure
of kings and nobles. But they also acted as papal agents for trans-
mitting the proceeds of papal taxation from England to Rome in the
shape (during the 13th and 14th centuries) of English wool. Thus they
became involved in the wool business, collecting the fleeces from the
large sheep farms (especially the Cistercian monasteries of Yorkshire
and Lincolnshire) necessary to Italy's cloth industry. As wool export
declined in face of the growth of a local English industry the emphasis
shifted to the export of bullion.

Meanwhile the Venetians and Genoese were bringing into England
luxury produce which roused all the English patriotic indignation
already crystallised in a theory of the balance of trade:

'The grete galleys of Venees and Fflorence
Be wel ladene with thynges of complacence
....
Trifles, trifles that litelle have availede
With thynges not enduryng that we bye.'

So the author of the *Libelle of Englysh Polycye* summed up his verse
essay in economic nationalism. 'Swete wynes', apes, 'marmasettes
taylede' and so on were the baits on the Italian hook. Meanwhile,
the Cotswolds were full of Italian merchants riding round buying
up England's golden fleeces, the bulwark of our industry.

Taxation, Papal economic oppression, industrial competition, the
ruination of the balance of trade—such were a few of the specifically
economic grievances which 15th-century propagandists and petit-
ioners laid at the door of the Italians. These were piled on top of
obvious distrust of a people who though sharing the same religion
spoke a different tongue and were already debited with a Latin repu-
tation for frivolity and deceitful cunning which turned into an Eliza-
bethan dogma. The charges were converted, in 1463, into an Act of
Parliament fostered by the gilds which forbade the import of a long
list of manufactured articles, mostly Italian by origin.

It is often pointed out that the banking and credit operations of the
Florentines passed by Tudor times into English hands: nevertheless,
many of the London merchant-bankers of Elizabeth's day were still
Italians, like her creditor, Sir Horace Palavicino, a Genoese come
to London via Antwerp, or his rival Spinola. Even almost down to the
Civil War, the Stuarts relied heavily on the services of Philip Bur-

lamachi (the 'great sponge' to whom Queen Henrietta Maria pawned the Crown Jewels) and Philip Calandrini, his brother-in-law.

By this time the London Italian bankers were as closely tied to the Low Countries—to Bruges and Antwerp especially—as to Florence or Genoa. We can move on to look at the position of another important but hardly popular alien minority to whom, in several senses, England was to owe much: the Flemings and Dutch.

The 15th-century author of the *Libelle* (probably a Bishop) had not restricted himself to attacking Italian weaknesses. The Scots—still a nation as foreign as any to the English—are depicted as boasters; but it was the Flemings' revolting table manners which came in for his strictures. Whence came this little observation? There were, especially from the 14th century onwards, plenty of small colonies of Flemings in England. Some—the larger men in London—were merchants, importers and exporters, but the majority in the London suburbs and the provinces were more likely to be weavers or at any rate cloth artisans of some kind. Indeed, an early version of the rise of the English cloth industry attributed it to Flemish weavers deliberately enticed here by Edward III. This was an exaggeration, but it is true that Flemish weavers were to be found widely spread, in eastern England especially, in the late Middle Ages. Lincoln, Stamford, Norwich, Bury, Colchester and other East Anglian towns and villages knew them, and when the Peasants' Revolt of 1381 occurred, East Anglian weavers were not slow to utilise the occasion to work off some old grudges against their immigrant competitors. Economic grievances aggravated xenophobic prejudice.

The 'strangers'

There was a measure of truth in the economic achievements attributed to the Flemings. Popular legend has always associated them with the towns and villages in eastern England which made something akin to worsteds rather than woollens. The trend was underlined in the new and spectacular wave of immigration of the 16th century. In retrospect the new age often looks like the beginnings of maritime and economic expansion; but to contemporaries it was more often a renewal of secular and ecclesiastical repression. The chief instrument of the latter was the Inquisition, which set in motion a whole chain of forced migrations. Spanish and Portuguese fled to Antwerp, Emden and Hamburg: then as Spain sought to impose her tyranny on the Low Countries, Jews and Protestants were forced into a new *diaspora* north into the Dutch Republic and westwards to England. These are only one of the many upheavals which, together with the 30 Years War, was to make Europe a scene of unprecedented population movements. Never had ordinary people in England or Holland found so many strangers and refugees in their midst.

The new influx of the 'strangers' began almost as soon as Elizabeth ascended the throne. In 1559, the Church of the Augustinian Friars in the City of London was assigned by the Privy Council to the 'strangers'. Similarly at Norwich in 1564 one church was assigned to the French-speaking Walloon refugees from the South Netherlands and another to the Dutch-speaking Flemings and Dutch from the North. They were licensed 'to exercise the faculty of making bays, says and other outlandish commodities as were not used to be made within this Realme of England'. The phrase was significant. When Archbishop Parker visited Sandwich in 1563 he noticed that the town contained many refugees—'French and Dutch or both'; they were both 'godly and busy'; or, as he later reversed the order '...profitable and gentle strangers [who] ought to be welcomed and not grudged at'. Ten years later, Queen Elizabeth herself went to see the port with its 'divers children, English and Dutch, to the number of 100 or six score all spinning of fine bay yarn'.

The nature of the *diaspora* is plain. From the towns and villages round Ypres, home of the New Draperies and radical Protestantism now threatened with the Inquisition and economic disaster by the Spaniards, the Protestant workers, mostly weavers, came to England. Sandwich seems to have been a reception centre from which many thousands of refugees passed on to London, Colchester, Norwich, Canterbury, Rye and other towns between the 1500s and 1600. Each immigrant had to be screened for what a later age would call 'security'. Cornelis Gelison, painter, born in Flanders, was pronounced by the Colchester bailiffs to be 'no fanatic, of honest conversation'. This was the standard certificate.

Steadily the 'strangers' spread over the face of (especially) East Anglia and the London suburbs. In all, probably a tenth of the most skilled workers of the Low Countries left the area we now call Belgium: possibly 100, 000-150, 000 in all. Of these, perhaps a quarter or a fifth found their way via Nieupoort or Ostend to Sandwich or the Thames Estuary. The total could have been 25, 000 to 30, 000.

The largest single concentration was in Norwich; here in the 1580s, about one-third of the city's population of 15, 000 were Flemish, Dutch or Walloon. They gave great stimulus, and may well have invented, the manufacture of the light, bright, cheap mixed worsteds called 'stuffs'—which not only made Norwich prosperous but came to form a flourishing branch of England's export trade. The rapidly growing suburbs of London absorbed even larger numbers but here they were spread more sparsely. A census of foreigners in 1618 suggests a figure of 10, 000. Colchester, with a watchful eye on the experiments of its Norfolk neighbour, appealed to the Privy Council to be also given a supply of these useful immigrants and did not regret the consequence. In 1612 the Bailiffs testified 'how beneficial the strangers of the Dutch congregation... have been and are unto our said Towne...'

They had replenished and beautified it, set the poor on work and generally increased its wealth 'without novelty, division or scandal' in religion.

This verdict is interesting. Perhaps because the government kept careful guard against 'fanatical' immigrants, the quarrels about religion were minimal—mainly family squabbles between Walloons and Flemings rather than Anglo-Dutch disputes. Even economic differences do not seem to have been serious. Norwich immigrant craftsmen sometimes caused trouble by invading the retail trade from which they were officially excluded. Colchester Dutch makers of bays and says did not always conform to the rules which compelled them to have their cloths stamped by their own Dutch inspectors for quality.

Only one real rumpus is on record. At the neighbouring village of Halstead, the 20 families of Dutch weavers had a frosty reception in the 1570s. They took up their beds and walked to Colchester. Too late the villagers of Halstead realised their error and petitioned for their return. The immigrants had joined the Colchester colony for good. Even in 1720 a local parson was still congratulating the town on its 'colony of Dutchmen planted...and exceedingly diligent to advance the trade' not only of Colchester but its satellite villages.

At its peak the Colchester colony probably contained some two thousand souls. As at Norwich the strangers maintained a more or less separate identity for approximately a century. But by the mid-18th century they had been largely assimilated. Names like Courteen (or Gurtin), Fromenteel, Burkin, Horn are still to be found in Norfolk and Suffolk, the vestigial traces of these old Dutch colonies. The London Dutch were probably more quickly assimilated, but the Austin Friars Church (rebuilt after complete destruction in the Second World War) continues. In the 18th century, the character of its congregation changed. The London Dutch who came with Dutch William in 1688 were merchants and bankers, wealthy capitalists like the Van Necks who financed England's wars, became baronets and later Irish peers and Governors of the Bank of England. It is always easier to assimilate at the top, as the history of, for example, Anglo-Indian and Anglo-Jewish social relations witnesses.

Fenland friction

Another large group of Dutch had a less fortunate history. They were the labour force of Walloons, Flemings and Dutch imported by the great Dutch entrepreneur and engineer, Sir Cornelius Vermuyden, himself a Zealander knighted by Charles I for draining the Fens from 1618 to 1640. Their contribution to the national welfare may have been substantial but the Fenmen were not convinced. All they knew was that their fishing and fowling had gone. At the Civil War they banded together, threw down the dykes painfully constructed by the immigrants, knocked the newcomers on the head and threw them into the water. But the work was never more than temporarily undone. Samuel Hartlib, a contemporary writer and himself an immigrant, claimed that the Fen drainage had added nearly 400,000 acres to England's good farmland.

The immigrant Netherlanders of Hanoverian London were closely connected with their fellow Protestants from France who arrived after their expulsion by Louis XIV in 1685. Probably between 50,000 and 100,000 of all those expelled came to England. Two years later, in 1687, about 16,000 were still in London living on charity but the large majority were already gainfully and novelly employed; mostly in London (where they may have represented 5 per cent or more of the population and a good deal more in an area like Spitalfields) they were also spread out into Essex, Macclesfield, Scotland and Ireland. The Spitalfields silk industry was as much a Huguenot invention as Norfolk stuffs were a Dutch one. Linen and its closely connected relation, paper (made from linen rags), were likewise their province. The Scottish and Irish linen industries owed a big debt to them; so did the Kent and Hampshire paper industry. (The Portals made paper for Bank of England notes till the present century.) Plate glass, rope-making, surgical instruments, and felt and beaver hats were a few of the numerous products they helped to establish in London and the provinces.

II   THE ERA OF TOLERANCE

From the Napoleonic Wars to the late 19th century nothing happened to disturb the belief generally held by Englishmen that the foreign immigrants into England had, by and large, made a beneficial contribution to society. Germans, Jews as well as Christians, continued to trickle into the chemical and scientific industries. Names like those of Brunner, Mond, Siemens, Haber, Levinstein, Nobel, Schuster and many others were witness to the scientific, technological and business skills which free immigration had conferred on England. They were, after all, hardly more 'foreign' than the Irish against whose Popery 18th-century mobs rioted in London and who in the 1840s flooded into the slums of Liverpool and Glasgow; nor even than the Scots of Lambeth and Bread Street who (if one anonymous scribbler of 1851, writing in the semi-jocular, semi-serious manner of Dr Johnson, is to be believed) still lived like a foreign colony in London. They were, he said, a secret people who kept to themselves, communing with their own relations and emerging into the daylight only on their national holiday to play the bagpipes and perform barbarous tribal dances. Above all, they were preachers, and that, he said, the English would not abide. But even they could not halt the progress of assimilation and emancipation of England's aliens. In

England Jewish disabilities were relatively slight. From 1830 they were steadily removed until the Act of 1858 removed their last legal handicap—their exclusion from Parliament.

Contribution to economic progress

Throughout 'modern' English history, the process of immigration had been inextricably mixed with the process of economic improvement. Indeed, without casting aspersions on the genuinely humanitarian motives which had animated the reception, for example, of the Huguenots, it is clear that successive governments had a shrewd appreciation of the economic and technological value of the immigrants whom they allowed and indeed encouraged to enter the country. In ages when industrial, and even commercial, skills were learned or transmitted not by handbooks or blueprints but from master to apprentice, there was only one way to promote and encourage the spread of technology: that was by personal instruction. William Cunningham, the Cambridge economic historian and one of the founding fathers of the study, drew attention to the strikingly similar industrial arts and practices to be found in widely separated parts of the world and asked how had this come about. By simultaneous and quite independent origination? Or by 'the conscious and deliberate transplantation of arts and institutions from one place to another'?[1] Surely the second was much more probable.

If it was by imitation, how did the process work? Transplantation could be effected if an article was exported and imitated: but this would probably happen only if the article was uncomplicated and easy to make. The Vikings may have imitated chain-armour from the types they had seen on trading expeditions to the Levant. Some recipes and formulae could be transmitted in literary form. A medieval monk (Cunningham pointed out) had written a treatise which claimed to explain all the processes used in the decorative arts known to the ancient and medieval world. But in general the only safe way to reproduce an article was to buy or hire the man who could work the process. And the clearest evidence that this frequently happened lay in the volumes of legislation by cities and gilds in the middle ages prohibiting the emigration of skilled craftsmen so as to guard the secrets they alone knew. Such legislation on a national scale continued in England until the repeal of The Prohibitory Acts in the 1840s.

The immigration of skilled artisans had been clearly linked in English history with economic progress. With the help of Flemings, Walloons, Dutch, Huguenots, new technologies had been imported, fostered, adapted; products had been manufactured which might

---

[1] W. Cunningham, *Western Civilization,* 1900, Vol. II, Appendix.

otherwise never have been available at all, or, if they were, necessarily imported from more advanced economies. That this process
of 'import substitution' and improvement had been speeded, if not
initiated, by immigrants is beyond doubt. Nor was the learning process limited to purely industrial skills. Knowledge of banking of all
kinds, of public and private finance had likewise benefited, especially
from Dutch and Huguenot and from the Sephardic Jews who came
to London from Holland in considerable numbers in 1688 and built
themselves a synagogue on the edge of the City at Bevis Marks.
When the 'City' presented a declaration of loyalty to George II on
the eve of the '45, between half and a third of the signatories bore
French, Dutch or Jewish names.

III RETURN OF INTOLERANCE

In the second and even third quarters of the 19th century, then, the
situation seemed nicely stabilised; many centuries of immigration
seemed to have been resolved in a satisfactory era of peaceful and
growing understanding, freedom and assimilation.

Jewish pogroms

The peace was shattered in the last quarter of the century by events
in Eastern and Central Europe. Beginning in Russia, and spreading
to Poland, Austria and Germany, a series of brutal pogroms, mas-
sacres and attacks against the Jews drove millions of them from
their homes. The largest number went to the United States but many
thousands came to Britain. The largest single concentration was in
the East End of London. In the 20 years before 1905, London's
Jewish population more than trebled, from 47,000 to over 150,000.
Smaller, but nevertheless sizeable, Jewish communities took root in
other provincial cities, especially in Leeds and Manchester.

The new arrivals posed a serious problem for local and central government, for they were mostly desperately poor. Trade unions,
already anxious over falling wages from the deepening of the 'Great
Depression' in 1886 onwards, were worried by the threat to the organisation of labour. Social workers were worried by the danger of slum
growth. Others, confusing cause and effect (as Cecil Roth, the historian of the subject has observed)[1] concluded that the new immigrants tended actually to create slums. Cunningham, writing in his
study *Alien Immigrants to England* in 1897, had praised immigration
as a process by which England had in the past learned much. But
had these latest immigrants (he asked) anything to teach in matters

---

[1] Cecil Roth, *Short History of the Jewish People*, 1947, Chs. XXIX
and XXX.

of technical skills or institutions? In any case, was not the day when England needed labour, skilled or otherwise, passing and giving way to an age when she needed the newest *machines*?

After some hesitation, Cunningham came down on the side of maintaining a liberal policy, largely because to stop immigration would have been a retrograde step for a country like England, with its long history of enlightened and humane welcome for immigrants. The doubts of others were less easily dispelled. On the contrary, they grew, and alarm culminated in the Aliens Immigration Act of 1905, which aimed to check and control but not to stop immigration. It remains the basis of our law on the subject today.

New industries

In the event, the new immigrants proved to be not so different from their predecessors of earlier centuries as the alarmists supposed. While the earlier immigrants like Ludwig Mond and Nobel were still revolutionising the British chemical industry. the newer arrivals tackled with equal success the problems of adapting British industry and trade to the conditions of mass production and consumption. The ready-made clothing industry rapidly expanding into one of the nation's largest trades, the cheap boot and shoe industry, cheap furniture manufacture and the cigarette industry were a few of their contributions to manufacturing industry. And, as if to answer Cunningham's query, one of their innovations was to replace hand-work by machinery: the sewing machine was the outstanding instance. Invented in the 18th century, it had been developed in the United States. It became one of the major innovations of the new Jewish garment industries.

The products of these new industries were siphoned through to the new consumers of the late Victorian and Edwardian age through chains of retail and general stores where the traditional commercial acumen of the immigrants found its outlet. In time, a share of the expanding wealth they created in trade and industry returned to society in the shape of charitable trusts for education, welfare and cultural activities.[1]

The persecutions at the turn of the century did not spell the end of the new phase of migration created by waves of anti-semitism. The process was repeated during the Nazi domination of Europe. Even

---

[1] E.g. Asa Briggs, *Friends of the People,* Batsford, 1956, gives the story of Lewis's stores. Charles Wilson, *Economic History and Historian,* Weidenfeld & Nicolson, 1969, Chapter 11, examines the shift in late Victorian England towards these new consumer industries in which the immigrants were especially active as entrepreneurs and workers.

now it is not clear that similar persecution will not recur—indeed
has not already recurred—in Russian and Russian-dominated territories.

IV   LESSONS FOR TODAY

History can rarely, if ever, indicate solutions to specific current
problems. The immigration problems of the 1960s are different from
the immigration problems of the past. In England down to 1939 they
were never more than sub-problems. Even the Jewish immigration
of the turn of the century goes unnoticed in a popular social history
like G. D. H. Cole and Raymond Postgate's *The Common People,*
written in 1936 when anti-semitism was on the rampage again. It is
given two lines in R. C. K. Ensor's perceptive and comprehensive
work, *The Oxford History of England 1870-1914.* Neither history
mentions the Aliens Act of 1905.

Medieval Jewry and religious intolerance

The immigrant-alien problem which has received most attention in
English history is that of medieval Jewry, culminating in total expulsion. Historiographically the explanation is no doubt that the great
age of the historian was also the age of liberalism, and an historian
did not even have to be very liberal to see the episode as a blot on
the national history. Yet the magnitude of the upheaval itself was in
inverse proportion to the problem, viewed rationally. The proportion
of Jews in any medieval city can never have reached anything comparable to the figure of, say, the Dutch and Walloons in Norwich or
Colchester or London in, say, 1600, or the Huguenots in 1700. In one
respect, these later immigrants were at a disadvantage in their relations with the native population, for many of them came knowing little
or no English. Yet Norwich managed to absorb and assimilate a Netherlands colony amounting to perhaps 30 per cent of its total population.
A hundred thousand French quietly and without fuss disappeared
into 18th-century England, perhaps half of them into London.

The differences are not far to seek. The Dutch and French were encouraged to come to England because influential opinion, including
that of government, saw advantages to the nation and to local areas
and interests in their doing so. If there were occasional local
jealousies or frictions (and there were) arising out of xenophobia or
the breach of economic conventions—corporate regulations governing
the conduct of trade, wage fixing, prices and the like—they were
settled or smoothed over by authority. In this process a decisive
factor was that the immigrants were not separated from the natives
by any wide gulf created by ethnic difference or religious belief.
Indeed, as Protestant victims of Roman Catholic persecution, they
started with the initial benefit of English sympathy.

On the other hand, everything conspired to multiply the difficulties of medieval Jewry. They were different by race and religion, and often easily distinguishable in appearance. Church and secular authorities combined to exclude them from normal economic activities and force them into the one—usury—which was universally condemned as an immoral form of exploitation. Thus even a tiny minority was in the end not absorbed or accepted because there was no will to absorb or accept. In so far as there was a genuine problem, it was religious not racial. The Jew willing to give up the faith of his forefathers and to be converted to the Christian faith could avoid most of the problems of his fellows, though only at the cost of his conscience, his dignity, and possibly his property. In the conditions of 20th-century thought, by turns sceptical, atheistical, materialist and gullible, it is difficult for most people to grasp the character and importance of religion in earlier ages. All the historian can do is to draw attention to religion as the strongest emotional element in the early immigrant problem, embracing and overshadowing even the economic and social elements in a context where toleration was unknown. Religion was behind much anti-Irish feeling in 18th- and 19th-century England. It still echoes harshly in Ireland even in 1970.

The problems which arose after the new influx of Russian and Polish Jews from the 1880s onwards still contained a religious element. The growth of toleration ensured that it was in no way comparable with the medieval problem. In itself, religion would not have been enough to give even the small opening to the Fascists which they tried to exploit in the 1930s. But taken *together* with the social, economic and linguistic issues there was enough to make assimilation difficult and encourage the growth of support for the Zionist ideal of a national home. The problems, e.g. of Manchester Jewry, were described penetratingly in Louis Golding's novel *Magnolia Street* (1932).

The only problems comparable in emotive power with religion in earlier ages have been the nationalism of the post French-Revolutionary era, and the combined problems of race and colour since the emergence, in the first half of the 19th century, of the slavery issue in the United States. Other largely economic problems can still create ugly situations; for evidence that neither race nor colour is the sole source of social hatred, observe the post-war refusal of British miners to accept Italian labour even in times when labour shortage was acute, and the proliferation of stories to support their refusal alleging a universal threat to the virtue of their wives and daughters.

Public opinion and the scale of immigration

The history of immigration in Britain is a series of kaleidoscopic patterns composed of ever-changing variables. Among them, probably the most important, and the most unpredictable, is what we call public opinion (not to be confused with 'informed opinion'). On all aspects of this problem, public opinion has moved visibly and recently at an increasing pace. Yet it would be dangerous to anticipate that the liberalism of the *avant-garde* will necessarily persist undisturbed or be quickly received by all, or that we can merely extrapolate the experience of the past. It may well be that the cautious Act of 1905 itself did help to create conditions, physical and psychological, in which the immigration issues down to 1945 became soluble. The dimensions of the current problem of coloured immigrants from the West Indies, India and Pakistan are, quantitatively, and qualitatively, enormously larger than those of any earlier problem.[1]

The first problem for the legislators is the welfare of all those, including immigrants already in Britain, for whom they are constitutionally responsible. The only general method for them to pursue suggested by a survey of the past is to win time; time for opinion at large, still suspicious and fearful of 'strangers', to be reconciled, time for the immigrants to achieve the education, skill, and increased social confidence which enabled the immigrants of 1900 and earlier not only to contribute to society but to become an essential component in it; i.e. the essence of the solution by assimilation (not necessarily personal/familial but social and political) is the *rate* of immigration. Given his opportunities, the immigrant has often displayed a special kind of vitality, as if movement singled out the most vigorous individuals or transplantation itself did something for them.

But the opportunities for change and growth may be killed if the attendant social problems—poverty, overcrowding, lack of education, grievance and unresolved prejudice—are allowed to multiply. The history of immigration in Britain suggests that such evils have multiplied most rapidly where immigrants have been concentrated too much together, where the *rate* of immigration has put too great

---

1 As a proportion of the total population, the Jews in medieval England never reached 1 per cent. The Dutch and Flemish may have slightly exceeded 1 per cent. The Huguenots may have represented between 1 and 2 per cent. Locally, as we have shown, the concentration could rise much higher. But it never came near the current figures for immigrants. In 1967, immigrant pupils represented 2.5 per cent of the total school population in Britain. In areas attracting larger concentrations of immigrants, over 13 per cent of the pupils in maintained schools were immigrant, mostly West Indian or Indian. In areas of specially concentrated immigration, like Wolverhampton, the percentage was much higher, reaching e.g. 43 per cent of the total pupils in Church of England primary schools.

a strain on the natural conservatism, and often positive xenophobia, of ordinary people, and where some irrational factor—be it religion or race or colour—has created an initial but obstinate bar to assimilation. Alongside the decline of intolerance based on religious belief in recent years, there has been a growing intolerance based on race and colour. The problems have been aggravated by the existence of great areas of poverty and backwardness in India, Pakistan and the West Indies in a world where improved communications and transport make it possible for the victims of backwardness to escape to the supposed paradise of the West. Hence the new ghettoes of industrial Britain.

In situations such as these, history certainly cannot offer solutions; often it can only offer commonplaces. But one general lesson can be learnt from the past. Governments can incite men to intolerance: they cannot bully them into tolerance.

2. IMMIGRATION UNDER 'ECONOMIC FREEDOM'

W. H. HUTT
Visiting Research Fellow,
Hoover Institution, Stanford University

THE AUTHOR

W. H. Hutt was born in London in 1899 and after First World War service in the RFC and RAF as a pilot (1917-19), studied at the London School of Economics, where he took the B.Com. degree. After four years in publishing, he joined the University of Cape Town in February 1928 as Senior Lecturer. In 1931 he was appointed Professor and Dean of the Faculty of Commerce, and later also Director of the Graduate School of Business, which he inaugurated. He was elected Professor Emeritus in 1965.

Visiting Professor of Economics, University of Virginia, 1966; subsequent appointments at Rockford College, Wabash College, Texas A & M University and the Hoover Institution, Stanford University (as Visiting Research Fellow). From September 1970 Visiting Professor of Economics at California State College.

Professor Hutt has published numerous articles and several books, including *The Theory of Collective Bargaining* (1930, republished in the USA 1954), *The Theory of Idle Resources* (1939), *Keynesianism— Retrospect and Prospect* (1963), and, for the Institute of Economic Affairs, *The Economics of the Colour Bar* (1964).

Large-scale movements of people, both within national areas and between them, give rise to perplexing ethical problems. The issues can be meaningfully studied only in the light of rigorous economics. Few ethical problems fail to touch crucial economic aspects. Ideas of morality influence the objectives of men; and these objectives—material or non-material—normally require means which are scarce and hence of economic value. Moreover, as Hume argued convincingly, the very idea of *justice* arises out of that attribute of things which gives them economic value. This is why the ethical factor has to be brought—at the outset—into a discussion of the causes and consequences of human migrations under 'freedom'. Yet attempts to unravel inconsistencies of thought in the field to be surveyed collide with the reality that even the most dispassionate and objective analysis, applying unchallenged ethical criteria, leads to conclusions which are apt at times to sound cynical, ironic or positively outrageous.

I. MOTIVES AND INCENTIVES

Forced and voluntary migration

The terms 'emigration' and 'immigration' are usually used to describe the *voluntary* movement of individuals to *preferred* national areas, for more or less permanent settlement.[1] Thus traditional usage excludes forced population transfers such as are brought about under slave-trading, or the transportation of convicts, or government-arranged population transfers intended to bring about eth-

---

[1] The words 'more or less' seem to be needed because persons admitted as immigrants are under no compulsion to stay, and they may finally decide to leave only after some time has passed. In the meantime they are included in the statistics of immigration. In practice, only a minority of resident aliens leave a country in which they had originally intended to stay.

The words 'permanent settlement' are necessary because temporary entrants, such as seasonal or other migrant workers, are not regarded as immigrants. Thus the Mexicans who enter the United States for fruit harvesting and the foreign Africans who enter South Africa from neighbouring territories to work for periods of varying length (in the mines, on the farms or in industry) are not immigrants.

nological or religious homogeneity.[1] But persons who leave a country to settle in another country so as to escape some disaster, say a famine, or to escape religious, racial or political discrimination, are also thought of as immigrants. Such migrants are not *commanded* to leave. They transfer to *preferred* national areas. Thus, the Huguenots were not *banished* from France in the 17th century. On the contrary, their departure, to avoid oppression, was illegal. But huge movements of emigrés who can be held to have been driven from the land of their birth and upbringing have occurred spasmodically through history, right down to the great influx of refugees into West Germany after the last war.[2] The essential feature of the population movements which we are to discuss, however, is that the persons who move can seldom be thought of as expelled from a country. That is, *we shall be considering certain consequences of the exercise of freedom of choice or judgement.*

Some contributors have tried to distinguish between 'push' and 'pull' factors as inducements to population transfers. Presumably, they feel there is a 'push' in persecutions, deportations, or where conditions are unjustly discriminatory for a particular group (either *via* legislation or the tolerance of private collusive action).[3] But could we say that people who, on retirement, migrate to a country of relatively low taxation are 'pushed' more by the high taxes at home than they are 'pulled' by the low taxes abroad? Or if they choose to migrate from a cold to a warm climate, could we say that they are 'pushed' more by the cold than 'pulled' by the warm climate? Or if people migrate to better earning opportunities abroad, would it ever have meaning to say that they are 'pushed' by the low earnings at home more than they are 'pulled' by the high earnings abroad? The answer is that, when we are concerned solely with preference between alternatives, the notions of 'pull' and 'push' are meaningless.

---

1 E. g., such exchanges of peoples as were effected in Eastern Europe after the First World War, *via* co-operation involving Greece, Turkey, and Bulgaria.

2 Movements *within* national areas may similarly be classified according to whether they are voluntary or forced. Large-scale population transfers within totalitarian countries, and the announced, but hardly yet implemented, separation of the races under the *apartheid* ('separate development') policy of South Africa, differ in principle from *voluntary* internal migrations, e.g., such as are very important today in the United States.

3 There may be nothing purposely unfair in circumstances which cause people of a particular class, race or religion to believe they will be able to find a better life under another regime.

Again, no distinction need be made between what some economists call 'economic' and 'non-economic' motives. When emigrants leave a country to escape religious intolerance, or to settle in an area where they can themselves impose intolerance (i.e., when they do *not* go because they are discriminated against in respect of opportunities for using their powers and assets in their land of birth), they *purchase* an objective at the costs of movement.

Indentured or deliberately recruited labour from abroad has to be included under the heading 'voluntary' in so far as those involved accept an honest contract of employment, elect not to return to their country of recruitment after the expiry of their contractual term, and are allowed to stay.[1] The binding of an indentured employee to an agreed term of employment may involve no departure from the free choice criterion. The recruiting entrepreneurs have financed the costs of movement in return for the willingness of the employee to bind himself for a specified period. As with other 'lock-in' contracts, the property relationship may be a means to the attainment of freedom and not a denial of it.

The term 'national area' needs some consideration. During the 19th century the whole British Empire was regarded as constituting a number of different races of one nationality, under one crown. And when the concept of the British Commonwealth of Nations became accepted, the idea of a common nationality survived. English, Scottish, Welsh and Irish settlers in the dominions were regarded as immigrants within the areas which accepted them, but they were thought of also as having an unquestioned right to move freely inside the Commonwealth. For some Commonwealth areas, this right appeared at times to resemble the right of Americans to move freely between states. Yet Indians (Hindus and Pakistanis) never had such a right automatically or effectively over all parts of the Commonwealth. Naturally enough, the idea of a common British nationality for peoples with such widely differing ethnological and cultural attributes led to troubles.[2]

---

1 Even when persons have been compulsorily deported, as were some 'vagabonds'—the chronically unemployed—from 18th century Britain, they have often shown no wish to return to their mother country when they have had the opportunity. They may then be held to have become immigrants by free choice, in spite of earlier deportation. In the case of the Chinese, indentured to serve in the South African mines in the early years of the century, their repatriation in 1907, following the outcry in Britain about 'Chinese slavery', was involuntary.

2 Difficulties arose on a small scale as early as 1843, after the British accepted responsibility for Natal; and far from being solved with the passage of time, the problems precipitated were

Growth of voluntary migration

The notion of voluntary migration as one of the rights of man gained acceptance as acquiescence in the remnants of absolute monarchical and authoritarian rule was in process of dissolution.[1] Because this transition accompanied (or was the outcome of) an age in which vast virgin areas of the earth were beginning to cry out for capital and people, the right to freedom of population movement seemed self-evidently reasonable. It was a corollary of a slowly emerging perception of the virtues of freedom of trade. The beneficence of voluntary migration was implicit in Adam Smith's *Wealth of Nations,*[2] with its recognition of the advantages of division of labour both within and among nations, and the general freedom of men to exercise preference as consumers and judgement as entrepreneurs. But probably with no direct inspiration from the great economist's work, the principle of the right of the individual to move freely, untrammelled by national boundaries, came to be enshrined in the American Declaration of Independence[3] and the Constitution of the French Republic of 1792.

The idea of deliberately promoting emigration from Western Europe, as well as permitting it, began to be considered as the rising cultural and material well-being of the people during the *laissez-faire* age caused, almost imperceptibly, changes in the criteria of bearable social conditions. Thus, possibly stimulated through the interest aroused by Malthus's contribution, governments became aware, early in the 19th century, of what seemed to be a downward population pressure on wage-rates towards or below a continuously rising conventional level of tolerable 'subsistence'. 'Surplus population', it was thought, might be profitably persuaded or assisted to transplant

---

aggravated as the consequences or prospects of voluntary migration disclosed themselves. Grave controversies centred around Australian policy; valiant attempts were made to solve the insoluble at the Imperial Conference of 1897; and the situation then debated inconclusively has continued to give rise to dilemmas down to this day. (Below, pp. 37-41)

[1] Locke's 'natural rights' thesis was, we believe, the first major enunciation of the principle.

[2] The word 'implicit' is essential because, although Adam Smith discussed the high wage-rates ruling in the colonies, he did not explicitly explain that the kind of restraints on human mobility over area which existed in his day were barriers to fruitful specialisation among the nations.

[3] British restraint on the *emigration* of artisans, dating from 1720, was one of the chief grievances of the American colonists.

itself in distant and more sparsely populated areas. This attitude
was explicit, in Britain at least, as early as 1819 when a Parliamentary Committee recommended not only the removal of surviving obstacles to emigration but also its encouragement.

Of course the costs of emigration from Europe to the great virgin
areas across the Atlantic were for many years enormously high, and
Adam Smith and his classical successors of the following century
assumed (in discussions of international trade) that there would be
relatively little population mobility between nations. Subsequent
history confirms the realism of that assumption. Until late in the
19th century, emigration from Europe lightened the 'pressure of population' to a very small extent indeed, although the rate of emigration
did tend to be stimulated in bad years (recession, or high food
prices) and to fall off in good years. Similarly, immigration very
seldom added more than a virtually negligible proportion to the population of any country—i.e., in relation to its natural rate of increase—
until the mass migrations which followed the development of steam-
ship routes and the opening up by railway and telegraph of the in-
teriors of North and South America and Australasia. Thereafter,
voluntary (sometimes assisted) population movements had a profound,
cumulative effect. Men, knowledge and capital spread over the under-
developed regions of the earth.

After the repeal in 1824 of the British law forbidding the emigration
of artisans, the notion that every individual possessed a natural
right to leave any national area to settle in another (provided he had
every prospect of being able to pay his way and not become a burden
on the community to which he moved) had become almost universally
and naively accepted in the countries influenced by 'classic liberalism'. Had it not been for serious practical difficulties experienced with migrations as the century advanced, the right of any person
to find his home and livelihood in any country he wished might have
come to be proclaimed even more explicitly as a fundamental freedom. It may, indeed, have crystallised as the sort of human right
which, in this century, could have been appropriately incorporated in
the terms of a United Nations charter. Yet we shall be forced to
the conclusion that it is not the kind of freedom which can be contemplated when the number of children a person may bear remains a
matter of individual preference, as most of us would agree it ought
to be.

Over-population and immigration

'If any people acts', wrote Edwin Cannan, 'as if its ideal of progress was, in Mills's picturesque phrase, 'a human anthill', it
is probably desirable that it should be confined within as
narrow limits as possible. It is better that it should learn that

over-population is an evil, and how to avoid it, in one country
or continent, than after extending it all over the world.'[1]

By 'over-population' Cannan meant a population magnitude in any
area larger than the optimum, i.e., larger than was conducive to the
maximisation of real income per capita.

Now the judgement Cannan shared with J.S.Mill implies that it is
'probably' justifiable ethically for the people of any area in which the
population is believed to approximate to the ideal or optimal magnitude to claim the right to exclude peoples whose entry can be reasonably expected, sooner or later, to upset the ideal. That is, it
justifies discrimination against such races as it is feared will multiply inordinately; and it implies further that the rulers of any nation
may legitimately admit only such immigrants as they predict will
be likely to contribute at least as much to the total material well-
being of the nation, or well-being in some other sense, as they will
withdraw from it.

We can best get to grips with the basic issues by considering the
implications of restraints on the area mobility of men in the light
of the ideals of 'classic liberalism'; and this means from the standpoint of those who advocate the planning of institutions with a view
to achieving the largest possible measure of 'economic freedom' in
all forms. Within any national area in which the ideals of democracy
and economic freedom are accepted, in the sense that they are at
least given lip service, we find that every person has the unquestioned legal right to move to where he believes the immediate or
future yield to his efforts (or those of his dependents) will be maximised.[2] But the normal beneficence of this right obscures the circumstances in which it might very well lead to intolerable situations.
The merit of the right stems from the incentive it creates for every
person of working age to locate himself and his family where he
predicts that his and his family's productivity—the value of their
contribution to the common pool of output in general—is likely to be
largest.[3] Moreover, the right of all persons in their entrepreneurial
capacity to choose those areas for investment in which they fore-

---

[1] Cannan, *Wealth,* 2nd Ed., p. 274.

[2] This right is seriously weakened in practice through trade
union enforcement of the 'rate for the job' and 'differentials'
('due relatives'). Minimum wage enactments have a like effect.
Apprenticeship restrictions, demarcations and the like, combined with the closed shop, although less important, tend in the
same direction.

[3] The value of a person's real income may include a 'psychic'
part, acquired at the expense of some portion of possible pecu-

cast that yields are likely to be maximised is a parallel right under the same 'classic liberal' philosophy. It means that assets will come to be located in areas where (to the extent to which forecasts turn out to be correct) their contribution to productivity will be largest.

This 'classic liberal' thesis does not imply that knowledge and foresight are perfect. Those who perceive the virtues of freedom of preference and judgement have reached their conclusions because they have reasoned, *inter alia*, from a recognition that the individual cannot always correctly forecast what is going to be best for him. Even when an entrepreneur is shrewd and accurately informed, his extrapolations may be wrong. The 'classical' theory of profit is based on a realistic insight into this source of risk. The case for 'economic freedom' is simply that, subject to two vital qualifications we shall emphasise below (Section II), it will be for the general advantage if every man is allowed to act in accordance with what he predicts will be for his advantage. And events have proved the practical wisdom of this precept in human migrations.

The incentives which cause men to emigrate are similar to those which lead to the export of commodities and capital. There are, for instance, gains to be won by movement from areas of relatively low productivity to areas of relatively high productivity; and motivations which can be classified under this heading are clearly dominant in voluntary migrations. Nearly always the prospective yields which have induced people to leave their native surroundings and their friends for lands of opportunity have been high;[1] and the prospects have seldom been wholly disappointing. Newcomers *have* succeeded, on the whole, in winning for themselves and their families higher material and psychic income. This is not surprising when we remember, in the words of a French economist, Daniel Bellet, that 'emigration in general makes towards the country where the need is sufficiently intense for it to become known at a distance'.[2] The percentage of immigrants who have returned voluntarily to their country of origin has throughout been small, in spite of frequent

---

niary income sacrificed. This might, for instance, occur when a person judges (to use Adam Smith's term) the 'net advantageousness' of £1, 000 p.a. in a pleasant, warm climate near the sea to be equal to £1, 400 p.a. in a cold smoggy industrial area.

[1] In the middle 1930s, for instance, real wage-rates for work of comparable skill appear to have been at least eight times as high in the United States as in countries like Esthonia and Bulgaria. (Colin Clark, *Conditions of Economic Progress*, 1940, p. 46.)

[2] De. Bellet, *Le Chomage et Son Remède*, F. Alcan, Paris, 1912, p. 18

lingering homesickness and temporary vicissitudes experienced.[1]
Hence the argument that the market for human services gravely
misleads and justifies exclusions from an area in the interests of
those excluded appears to have no substance. Voluntary immigrants[2]
have been largely young people, quite prepared to invest at risk their
careers, their way of life and such savings as accompany them. They
have accepted a calculated sacrifice of security at home as well as
the breaking of family and community ties.

It is possible that, in earlier periods, the rewards to the emigrants'
enterprise were *relatively* higher than they could be anywhere today.
But even in the days when the average gains were most impressive,
persons who resented the alien influx still argued that immigrants
should be excluded in their own interests. 'These miserable newcomers', said one writer, 'find themselves worse off than they were
before, ... the only result is that they intensify the awful struggle
for existence.'[3] If the newcomers' *ultimate* well-being is the criterion, the first part of this assertion stresses an unimportant exception. The second part of the assertion points to, although it exag-
gerates, a possibility which may be of enhanced importance in the
presently emerging era.

The areas which have acted as a magnet have tended to be those
which have possessed or have been *simultaneously accumulating*
complementary assets; and the strongest attraction has been from
countries with under-developed natural resources, a growing volume
of technological equipment, a growing availability of administrative
and technical skills, and a sufficiently large segment of the economy
in which strike-threat or political influence on the pricing of the
product of labour has been absent or weak.

II. CLASSIC LIBERALISM QUALIFIED

Exploitation and social costs

We must now turn to what we termed above two vital qualifications
of the 'classic liberal' thesis. The first is obvious—that the indi-

---

[1] There is a large literature stressing the disappointments and
hardships of immigrants which drove many (but a small proportion) to return. Much of this literature is mentioned in W. S.
Shepperson's study of English repatriates from the United States,
Emigration and Disenchantment, University of Oklahoma Press,
1965.

[2] 'Voluntary' here means those who have left for reasons other
than the avoidance of persecution or discrimination.

[3] W. H. Wilkins, *The Alien Invasion,* Methuen, 1892, p. 1.

vidual shall be restrained from defrauding[1] or exploiting[2] others—just as he is prevented from robbing them. The second is that the phenomena of 'externalities' (or 'social cost' and 'social benefit') shall be taken into the reckoning. 'Externalities' refer to the effects of the exercise of free preference and judgement by individuals: (a) harm, termed 'social cost', to other parties (including the community generally);[3] or (b) the loss of assets ('public goods'), the services of which people as a whole *would* demand sufficiently if the cost amounted to a small enough sacrifice of other things, but which cannot be cheaply enough provided unless they •re financed through taxation, so that a possible 'social benefit' is lost under free-market financing.[4] We shall have to decide whether any modifications of the case for the beneficence of free movement, due to these factors, are important.

In practice, harm caused to third parties by persons exercising free choice and judgement is seldom to be explained as 'social cost'. For instance, the dissolution of a colour bar, although it causes a detriment to the race which had been protected by the bar, represents the achievement of more market freedom and not a condition which ideals of freedom require to be rectified. Similarly, a capital-economising or labour-economising managerial ingenuity or technological invention is likely to injure *some* persons; but it is through

---

1 Frauds by land salesmen have been alleged. Shipping lines have been accused of painting an unduly favourable picture of prospects in the developing areas in order to attract 'steerage' passengers.

2 'Exploitation' can be defined as any *deliberate* action, individual or collusive, which reduces the income or prospects of one or more other persons, otherwise than through (a) the dissolution of some privilege formerly possessed by the persons harmed or (b) the introduction of some economy or preferred output.

3 Clear examples are a noxious industrial process located where it injures, or prevents the most economic location of, another industry producing food; or where pesticides raise agricultural outputs but exterminate fish in rivers and nearby oceans.

4 The 'social benefit' situation exists when some prospective beneficiaries might otherwise count on not having to pay for amenities enjoyed, so that the yield promised to investors is insufficient to make provision of the amenities profitable. A clear case is that of street lighting and police protection where a service for one person is necessarily a service to another. For simplicity, we have described an extreme case. The effect could be that consumers received a more expensive service—i.e., less of the service than could be enjoyed if it were collectively provided.

the attainment of outputs and other objectives with a smaller use of capital and labour that all 'economic progress' has been won.[1]

An influx of immigrants with the qualities likely to add materially to the well-being of the majority of a population (that is, to increase society's real *per capita* income) may certainly compete to the detriment of a minority. But only if this can be said to cause an unjust sharing of the benefits and the burdens, because a minority of investors and workers may be grievously hurt as society prospers, is there any problem which even resembles that envisaged under the term 'external diseconomies'. Even in such a case there is really no 'social cost' or 'diseconomy' at all. Changes which affect certain incomes adversely and unpredictably may cause *individual income security* to become either (i) a product sought at a cost through insurance against unforeseeable contingencies, or (ii) a collectively-sought objective for all individuals, involving a collective cost.

The true problem of 'social cost' as a factor in the economics of migration is, we suggest, encountered in two principal forms. The first is met when immigration tends to create over-population in an immigrant-receiving country (in spite of freedom of movement tending to maximise aggregate real world income per capita—the population of the world being assumed constant). The second concerns the clash of cultures which seems inevitable under free, non-discriminatory immigration in an era of racially prejudiced proletariats. This reality has to be contemplated with uninhibited intellectual courage. No detached student can fail to observe how profitable politicians find it today to exacerbate the hatreds and resentments which the colour-intolerance of the masses engenders. In terms of votes, it is much more rewarding to exploit racial stupidities than to attempt to ameliorate or eradicate them. We shall return to this issue[2] after trying to classify into an intelligible simplicity the heterogeneous motivations which curb the voluntary movement of peoples.

Reasons for restricting immigration

Restrictions on immigration may be imposed for six broad reasons:

    (i)   through the people of an area resolving to protect certain

---

[1] Economies *followed by co-ordination of the economy through price and wage-rate adjustment* add to the source of demands in the aggregate. Labour-economising inventions in any set of activities raise the real value of wage offers in non-competing activities generally. Capital-economising inventions also tend to raise the real value of wage offers in the activities in which they are introduced.

[2] Below, pp. 39-43.

of their occupations from competition (that is, from the price consequences of the prospective outputs which the immigrants might supply);

(ii) (a quite different case) through the wish to protect the per capita real income of the nation;

(iii) through the wish to avoid the sociological disharmonies referred to in the preceding paragraph;

(iv) to keep out 'undesirables';

(v) to exclude such immigrants as are thought likely to send over-generous remittances to their homelands or, after accumulating sufficient savings, to return to their native land for retirement;[1] and

(vi) for 'political reasons'.

Case (i) provides a very important motivation. It is, however, completely indefensible in terms of the 'classic liberal' ideal which is here our standard and hence need not be further considered. Cases (ii) and (iii) concern issues which, we think, are properly envisaged under 'social cost', although they refer to different circumstances. Case (vi) involves factors which may bear on the other cases, but is sometimes dominant.

Reasons for restricting emigration

Restraints on emigration have been imposed far less often than restraints on immigration. There have been a variety of reasons:

(i) to prevent citizens from escaping obligations (e.g., attempted tax-evasion, debt-evasion, leaving dependants in destitution, avoiding conscription, etc.);

(ii) to protect those who might find that the land they set out to enter will refuse them admission;

(iii) to prevent the export of capital in the form of the emigrants' savings, or remittances sent to them by friends or relatives as they are finding their feet;

(iv) to achieve the intellectual isolation of a proletariat by an 'iron curtain';

(v) (the most defensible reason for restraining emigration) to check the loss of some part of the *human* capital of a nation;

---

1 With a few exceptions, the amounts of capital transfers of this sort have been of negligible importance in relation to capital movements as a whole.

(vi) to maintain a large or increasing population as a source of national power.

A general *discouragement* of emigration, and a prohibition of it in the case of artisans, was characteristic of the Mercantilist era. It involved the reasons (v) and (vi). The Mercantilists thought of emigrants as capital, a source of or means to 'wealth'. They perceived realistically also that nations with large populations possessed power and hence a form of security; and their way of thinking about national power ought not to be dismissed uncritically. There are independent-minded students of world trends who are uneasy because, in the countries with the highest living standards and with the strongest armaments, the rate of replacement of parents is tending to decline. Thus Colin Clark regards it as ominous that, if we can extrapolate from present trends, in half a century we shall have 'a world dominated by the Asian countries with India and China in the lead, and Pakistan and Indonesia as the runners-up'.[1] But we shall here ignore the question of how a 'classic liberal' policy would be affected if such forecasts were accepted and viewed as dangers.

The notion of *wealth* as the well-being of the people, that is, as what Adam Smith was later to call 'a plentiful subsistence for the people', was only vaguely conceived by the Mercantilists; but they do seem to have discerned that the parents of emigrants had invested in their upbringing, while masters had invested in the completion of the emigrants' education and technical training. The 'nation' should not permit the loss of this capital.

If the problem is today little discussed, there are two explanations. First, apart from a general tightening of immigration controls in the world, the likelihood of emigrants finding sufficiently remunerative employments overseas to justify the necessary risks has been considerably reduced through trade union exclusiveness.[2] Secondly, for similar reasons, there is hardly a government today which would not

---

[1] Colin Clark, *National Review,* May 1969, p. 485.

[2] The remarkable ease with which huge numbers of immigrants with many different languages, religions, cultures and degrees of literacy, were absorbed into the American economy before the First World War appears to have been due not only to the presence of a wide range of non-union occupations but to the absence of minimum wage laws. The virtual certainty of finding a source of income immediately, if only in unskilled work, while looking for more permanent openings, provided an important form of social security for immigrants. They could always discount prejudice and initial inferiority in order to ensure access to consumers. Immigrants' wage-rates often ranged from between half and three-quarters of the Americans' wage-rates in the sort of occupations they could find. (J. Isaac, *Economics of Immigration,*

welcome the loss of 'surplus labour' by emigration, whether in the
form of artisans or labourers. In nearly the whole of the 'western
world', strike-threat pressures are continuously forcing wage-rates
to heights which would cause a cumulative decline in activity with
labour displacement at all levels, if it were not for creeping, crawl-
ing, chronic inflation (which crudely mitigates the resulting chaos
in the labour market). In these circumstances, any incentive for
governments to monopsonise a people's skills has been dissolved.

Supposed 'surplus population' in this situation cannot be accepted
as evidence of over-population, of course. An under-populated country may have beggars, paupers or large numbers subsisting on
'welfare' services and handouts. The widespread prevalence of
dependency on relief checks in the United States, at real income
values which would be accepted as unimaginable affluence among at
least 90 per cent of the world's population, is obviously no proof of
over-population. Nor is a condition of recession or depression. But
in these circumstances governments are unlikely to restrain
emigration!

Theoretically, if clear-cut investment in a would-be emigrant (by
others than the would-be emigrant himself) can be shown to have
occurred, the solution acceptable under 'classic liberal' criteria is
a 'lock-in' contract. It could be concluded either with a 'commercial'
undertaking or with a government and cover a period as arbitrary
as the duration of patents and copyrights.

This case is probably of no practical importance; yet apart from it
there is no justification for any governmental use of monopsonistic
power to restrain international labour mobility. In all other cases,
the defensible reaction, if the loss of the would-be emigrant's skills
or labour is believed likely to diminish the real income of the rest,
is simple: bid more than the foreigner.[1]

---

p. 35.) (More than half the Portugese and Italian, and more than
one-quarter of the Greek and Jewish immigrants, were illiterate
during the first decade of the century.)

After the Wagner Act of 1935, which strengthened the closed shop
and encouraged the industry-wide use of the strike-threat, immigration into the United States, which had been declining slowly for
other reasons, fell off rapidly, while between the periods 1925-29
and 1935-39 the percentage of immigrants in the categories 'professional' and 'commercial' (non-unionised) increased from 5.9%
to 18.8% and from 2.9% to 19.6% respectively. On the other hand,
the percentage in the 'labour' category ('skilled' and 'unskilled')
fell from 86.4% to 56.7%. (*Ibid.*, p. 187.)

[1] This is how Brazil and the Argentine are now thinking of tackling
the problem of the 'brain drain' of scientists to the United States.
Venezuela has already adopted that policy with success.

The counterpart of politically-motivated restrictions on *emigration* such as we have just noticed is, perhaps, restrictions on the *immigration* of persons who are classed as 'undesirables' *for political reasons* (that is, together with 'hippie' types, illiterates, mental defectives, drug addicts, persons with a criminal record, or those who are deemed likely to become a public charge). As long as the 'cold war' remains a reality, it would be thought reckless of the countries of the so-called 'free world' to risk 'red penetration' and admit immigrants from the communist areas without the most careful screening. The political factor can, however, take many forms and there are examples in which immigration has been either discouraged or assisted on *purely* political grounds, in the sense that the expected effects upon votes for the political party in power, or upon the balance between different races or language groups, have provided the primary motivation.[1]

The costs of 'over-population'

We can now return to the problem of 'social costs' in the form of

---

The reader must not forget that our acceptance of the ethical standards of classic liberalism is paramount. A totalitarian country would look at things differently. The ruling establishment might exploit the monopsonistic power of the State first to ensure cheap skills and cheap labouring work, or secondly, as we have already noticed, to prevent the people governed from acquiring knowledge of conditions in less totalitarian societies.

[1]   The best example known to the writer concerns South Africa. After the Boer War, Lord Milner successfully encouraged an enormous immigration of British in order, the Boers alleged, to increase the voting power of the English-speaking section against the Afrikaans-speaking section. After the Second World War, General Smuts' Government inaugurated a highly successful policy of actively attracting immigrants from Europe, again (so Afrikaner politicians alleged) in order to acquire additional voters for Smuts' United Party, and in order to rob Afrikaners of the jobs to which they were entitled. When the Government changed, the Nationalist Party had to make a show of reversing the injustices it had alleged in its propaganda, and for the three years 1949-51, net immigration dwindled to a negative magnitude. Then, from 1952 onwards, recognising the political folly of shutting off voluntary immigration of Whites in a land in which non-Whites (mainly unenfranchised) formed a large majority, a complete reversal of policy was adopted. Since then immigration has boomed.

'over-population', which may be incurred through immigration.[1] The fact that *ceteris paribus* the employment of wage-earner immigrants cheapens labour in the particular activities in which they find openings does not mean that they necessarily reduce the real value of wage offers as a whole any more than the introduction of labour-economising innovations can be expected to have this effect.[2] With labour-saving *economies,* the aggregate effect tends always to raise the real yield to effort in general. This has been true without exception ever since the invention of the spade, the wheel and the lever. Thus, the reason why 'put and carry' work in the western world can today command perhaps ten times as much in real terms as it could, say, a century and a half ago, is that the process of economising-displacement has permitted given outputs to be achieved with fewer workers. Whenever it is possible to reduce the rate of recruitment of labour or to lay-off labour in any activity while maintaining or raising output, labour (and some co-operant resources) will have been released for the production of *additional real* income. It is this process which, together with capital-economising ingenuities, constitutes the dynamic factor in economic progress—technological advancement which multiplies the wages-flow. The phenomenon is comprehensible only when it is understood (a) that the co-ordinative process (price and wage-rate adjustment) must follow economies achieved if the benefits are to be realised immediately or early; and (b) that the cheapening of any individual output is the process through which the producers of that output make an enhanced contribution to the source of demands for all non-competing outputs.

To show the relevance of this special formulation of 'Say's Law', it will be useful to enunciate what may be called 'the basic law of wages':

> *Given any population of working age, and in the absence of monopsonistic exploitation,* the aggregate flow of *real* wages will be maximised, and inequality in the distribution of the wages flow will be minimised, when every wage-earner is offered and accepts the *lowest wage-rate* necessary to acquire his services.[3]

---

1 The 'social costs' of over-population cannot of course be envisaged in terms of 'real income' per head alone. Even in so vast a country as the United States, continuously worsening pollution of rivers, lakes, sea and atmosphere are phenomena of population pressure, although eradicable at a cost.

2 Above, pages 27-28.

3 The writer hopes in a forthcoming book to answer possible objections to this crucial economic law which, because it is almost

The law states a special case of a general proposition which is less likely to be questioned:

> The aggregate flow of real income will be maximised when entrepreneurs acquire all productive services needed (those of men and of assets) at least cost.

The general proposition simply means that, to the extent to which the 'least-cost' aim is realised, each human objective will be achieved at the minimum sacrifice of other objectives.

'The basic law of wages' implies, in the present connection, that whether any growth in population of working age beyond the optimum happens to have been caused mainly by immigration or mainly by 'natural increase',[1] the adverse effect upon *per capita* wages will be greater the more the pricing of labour departs from the wages-maximising ideal. In other words, whether any increase in aggregate labour supply which under otherwise ideal conditions would cause a crude average wage-rate[2] to fall, happens to be due to the entry into employment of juveniles or of adult immigrants, any adverse effects upon *per capita* income will be aggravated by a failure to price the additional labour in accordance with the 'basic law'.

III. THE ETHICS OF RESTRICTION

We can now ask: Is there any *ethical* justification for a nation to exclude aliens who could improve their earning power by entering as immigrants? *Ought* not all nations voluntarily to incur the hardships of over-population? Are not immigration restrictions otherwise defending privilege? In the following paragraphs we suggest an answer to these questions.

---

everywhere ignored in policy-making, may well be mainly responsible for frustrating the achievement of this generation's ideals.

[1] Economists have at times explicitly discussed the influence of natural increase and immigration upon one another. Malthus, for instance, originally thought (early in the 19th century) that it was purposeless to try to mitigate poverty by encouraging the emigration of 'surplus population' because the reaction would be an offsetting rise in the rate of natural increase in the home country (although he qualified this belief later). F. A. Walker (at the other end of the century) believed that the great immigration into the United States, which was approaching its peak when he wrote (1896), had been more or less neutralised throughout by a decline in the rate of natural increase at home.

[2] Aggregate wages divided by the number of wage-earners.

A well-known book on monetary theory, to simplify an issue, begins by asking the reader to imagine a society where the only commodity is manna, dropped on the earth with no process of production. A similar approach may perhaps assist the present exposition. Let us envisage a world in which manna is the only food and the only valuable commodity; that it is distributed unequally but regularly over the earth's surface (like rain); that the movement of people from one country to another is initially forbidden; that the ratios between the magnitudes of population and manna supplies differ in different countries, so that in some parts of the world people are well-fed and live long, whereas in other parts they suffer continuously from hunger and have short life expectations; and that the sole cause of varying population manna ratios in different countries (with the consequent grave contrasts in material well-being) is that people in the well-fed countries individually plan the number of births while those in the undernourished countries rely upon Malthusian checks.

Suppose now that the leaders in the hunger-suffering countries indignantly demand 'living room' and call for the removal of prohibitions on movement, so that the sufferings of their people shall be mitigated. In such circumstances, would not all moralists agree that the people of the well-nourished countries, having attained their envied condition through a tradition of concern for the welfare of their prospective progeny and the exercise of responsible foresight, are righteous (although harsh towards the innocent) in their determination to exclude 'surplus population' from the hunger-ridden communities which have failed to develop or copy that tradition?

Impact of technology

A parallel situation exists in the real world, not only in respect of the relation between population magnitudes and the yield to labour co-operating with natural resources (corresponding to manna), but equally in relation to the yield to labour in co-operation with the stock of man-made resources. There are diminishing returns from labour applied to both kinds of resources, although this may be countervailed (or more than countervailed) by increasing returns due to economies of scale in co-operative activity.[1]

The case for restraints on immigration is even stronger when diminishing returns from the application of labour to man-made

---

[1] It is through *increasing* returns to work that, up to a point, an influx of immigrants into a country may be to the advantage of the majority of the community which accepts them. We must *reckon separately* any valuable knowledge, teachable skills, enterprise or capital which may accompany the immigrants. These things constitute *additional* advantages.

resources (plant, equipment, tools, etc.) are brought into the reckoning. *For man-made resources are the outcome of traditions and
institutions* which encourage thrift, enterprise, industriousness and
self-improvement, and permit profitable investment (of domestic
savings and capital attracted from abroad) into assets of the most
effectively wage-multiplying type. The required institutions include:
integrity of government, independent courts, the rule of law, and
certainly that nationalisation, taxation, or use of the strike-threat will
not be used to confiscate capital invested in non-versatile assets. [1]

The objections to sharing the benefits with people from a community
in which these virtues, and responsibility in breeding, are not encouraged or even discouraged, fall into the same category as the
objections of far-seeing humanitarians to policies which, *within a
country,* exploit the thrifty for the benefit of the improvident, take
from the industrious for the benefit of the indolent, tax the enterprising for the advantage of the cautious, and penalise those who
have developed their powers in order to help those who have not.
But because would-be immigrants are not voters in the countries
they seek to enter, the *reasonableness* of limitations on entry is more
easily understood.

In enacting such limitations, direct account is seldom taken of any
harmful consequences upon the welfare of those excluded. The implication is that governments and other leaders in foreign countries
should assume their own responsibility for creating conditions conducive to the well-being of their people. And when the voluntary or
involuntary largesse of taxpayers provides unearned income for the
'deserving poor', the case for restraint of immigration is extended.
For in becoming residents and potential voters, the newcomers
would add to the liabilities of taxpayers.

In sparsely populated countries, however, if other conditions are
favourable, economies of scale are likely to render an increased
population of working age profitable to the existing population. In
these circumstances, additions through immigration are likely to be
more advantageous than equal additions due to natural increase. For
adult immigrants add to the number of active persons without the
costs of their upbringing and training having to be incurred, while
they may bring capital, knowledge and teachable skills. Such countries will often assist immigration and advertise the prospects.

---

[1] Non-versatile (i.e. 'specific') assets usually multiply the aggregate wages yield more than the versatile form. But they are
relatively exploitable by the strike-threat, and hence make up a
much smaller proportion of the aggregate stock of assets than
they would if wage-rates were determined under the social discipline of the market.

Conflict of interests: capital v. income

The phrase 'profitable to the existing population' ignores, of course, the possibility that what is to the advantage of some may be to the disadvantage of others. For instance, *ceteris paribus* the owners of assets as such (the 'capitalists') will *always* gain from an increase in the population of working age.[1] Hence there can be a real conflict of interest. And in practice opposition to immigration *does* arise mainly from the wage-earning classes. Yet skilled artisans also will find an increase in the numbers of unskilled and semi-skilled workers to their advantage, if there is no prospect of the unskilled coming to learn their skills and competing.

Suppose, for example, the Australians could have been guaranteed in the last century that non-Whites (Polynesians, Chinese, Indians, Japanese and so forth) admitted to their country would be strictly confined, by legal enactment (say, in the form of South African 'job reservations') to work on the plantations and farms, or in the mines or in domestic service. The insistence upon a 'White Australia' policy would then probably have found little support in white labour circles.

A policy of that kind was inconceivable, of course. It would have required the withholding of common roll electoral rights from the non-Whites. Nevertheless it would almost certainly have meant that the present white population of Australia would have been at least double while enjoying an incomparably higher average standard of living; and millions of Polynesians, Indians, Chinese and others (whether admitted as indentured labour or not) would have gained even more than the Whites in comparison with what they could have expected in their homelands. To refer to just one form of development which it is reasonable to assume would have been experienced under such a policy, Australian mining output would have been prodigious in relation to what has been achieved.[2]

The principle that non-competing groups will be welcome sometimes applies from the opposite angle. Thus, it will be to the advantage of unskilled workers (e.g., tribal Africans being gradually absorbed into modern economies) that skilled immigrants shall be attracted.

---

1   In a prospering and thrifty society, the bulk of the workers tend to become owners of assets in some degree; but among the majority the yield from effort and skill will considerably exceed the yield from property. Hence in this respect the conflict of interest remains.

2   The purpose of this illustration is solely to draw attention to the complexities which have to be brought into consideration. The judgement of posterity will surely be that the 'White Australia' decision was wise in the extreme.

Quite apart from the fact that the skills which accompany the immigrants may be taught and learned, *the current exercise* of those skills creates better opportunities for the rest of the labour force. In many under-developed territories, *for rapid progress to occur* towards an accumulation of the stock of assets needed to multiply the wages-yield, the native peoples must be allowed initially to price their labour sufficiently cheaply (a) to leave the prospect of relatively high yields to foreign or domestic investment and (b) to permit co-operant executive ability and skilled labour needed to be bid away from elsewhere in the world. Some African states seem, indeed, to be trying to resurrect the colonial policy of attracting and retaining white executives and officials trained for responsibility, and white technicians and artisans,[1] side by side with a gentle dissolution of such tribal customs as obstruct productive efficiency.[2]

The conflict of interest we have been stressing concerns population magnitude; and it is most acute between property owners as a whole and earners as a whole. It is just as much for the advantage of those whose income is the yield to assets (including profits) that there shall be as plentiful a labour supply as possible (and unrestrained immigration or unbridled breeding may cause this)[3] as it is for wage-earners as a whole to encourage a low rate of interest due to net accumulation of assets from domestic savings or the importation of capital.[4] When the propertied classes (other than politicians

---

[1] Our reference to 'Whites' here is realistic. American Negroes qualified for responsibility or possessing skills would be more expensive than Whites from Europe. In the present decade, Asiatics would be even more disliked in the African territories (perhaps unjustly) than the British, French, Portuguese or Belgians ever were.

[2] Such a country could hardly be expected to welcome an influx of still primitive tribesmen from neighbouring territories where a policy of equal enlightenment was not being followed. A situation of that kind may partly explain the troubles which broke out between the Somali nomads and Kenya following the relinquishment of colonial responsibility. The nomadic Somalis had traditionally ignored boundaries when, in the trail of rains and grass, they fought for survival by trampling with their cattle and camels over neighbouring territories.

[3] Fear of political instability due to over-population may provide a different motivation.

[4] This is because, in a given state of technology, the application of further increments of capital to a given stock of natural and man-made resources and a given volume of labour is also subject to diminishing returns.

or those whose fortunes depend on the favour of politicians) support immigration restrictions, it is presumably for disinterested reasons, or perhaps for reasons which (valid or otherwise) most of us would say are worthy. And even when the investing and executive classes cannot be exonerated from the charge of 'racist' activation, they can at least claim that the ends for which they press (e.g., 'race purity') entail a sacrifice of *pecuniary* benefits on their part.

The 'White Australia' policy

The point can be illustrated by a comparison of the attitudes of 'labour' and 'non-labour' support for the 'White Australia' policy at a crucial point in history, namely, at the turn of the century. Strong pressure on Australia for the admission of non-Whites was then being applied by the mother country. The British Colonial Office was particularly averse to any policy which might have appeared as a slur on Japanese and Indians. And any general exclusion of Indians certainly clashed with declared imperial tradition. The principle, which was enunciated in 1843, had seemed eminently reasonable in an age of *laissez-faire*. It insisted that '... There shall not be in the eye of the law any distinction or disqualification whatever founded on mere distinction of colour, origin, language or creed'.[1] By the end of the century the idea had survived. It was reiterated unequivocally by Joseph Chamberlain at the Imperial Conference of 1897. The Empire, he stated, 'makes no distinction in favour or against race or colour'. Referring to the problems facing the Australians, he 'appealed eloquently for tolerance and respect to be given to their 300 million Indian fellow subjects who though alien in race possessed a rich and ancient culture'.[2]

In spite of Chamberlain's eloquence, however, all three Australian political parties at the turn of the century (Labour, Protectionist and Free Trade) 'remained unshaken in their declared resolve to maintain the "White Australia" policy...'.[3] But *non-Labour* support for the exclusion of certain races, especially Orientals, was motivated by forebodings of future sociological and political troubles which, in the light of working-class reactions at that time, seemed to be inevitable in a multi-racial community with wide ethnic and

---

[1] This principle was asserted in a Proclamation by the Governor of Natal, Sir George Napier, when the British took responsibility for Natal, in 1843.

[2] A. T. Yarwood, *Asian Migration to Australia*, pp. 12-13.

[3] *Ibid.*, p. 12.

cultural diversity.[1] One special fear was that a situation could emerge like that which had developed in the 1890s in South Africa, where a large population of voteless foreigners had settled in the Transvaal—the 'Uitlanders'.[2] Another fear was of a large group of racially-defined immigrants appealing to the government of their country of origin for protection against imagined (or real) injustices; or, in the event of an attempted invasion, forming what this generation calls a 'fifth column'.

Such apprehensions, which were found among supporters of the non-Labour parties, had to be balanced against frequent expression of respect by them for the cultures and civilisations of Japan, India and China. The leaders of the Free Trade Party, in particular, pleaded for racial tolerance. They urged a humanitarian approach and stressed international goodwill. Moreover, they had strong misgivings about the possible destruction of existing industries which were already employing and dependent upon non-Whites. There was indeed pressure from non-Labour circles for the admission of Polynesians and others, under indenture, for the development of the area north of the latitude of Capricorn. But while the leaders of the Free Trade Party were clearly aware of the material sacrifices which the 'White Australia' policy demanded, their support for it remained unequivocal, a fact which did not prevent them deploring the crude racism of Labour Party spokesmen.[3]

The Labour Party leaders and organs, on the other hand, echoed the deep hostility and resentments which the Australian labouring and artisan classes had come to feel towards non-Whites. In 1901, the leader of the Labour Party, referring to the use of education tests for admission of the Oriental, remarked bluntly, 'the more educated, the more cunning he becomes'. And Labour journals, such as the

---

[1] Most countries with populations of European origin have excluded Orientals after having initially allowed them in. In the United States Chinese were excluded from 1882 and Japanese from 1908. The fertility of these Orientals (who have proved good Americans) has been very much greater than the average.

[2] Troubles with this alien element had angered the Boers into a declaration of war against the British, who were demanding what they thought was justice for the high-taxed but politically unrepresented foreigners who had settled on the gold fields.

[3] *Ibid.*, p. 3. The Free Trade Party was, however, accused by the Labour Party of hostility to the 'White Australia' policy. The official support of the policy by the Free Traders was alleged to be a cynical attempt to capture the labour vote. (*Ibid.*, p. 33.)

Sydney *Bulletin,* appealed throughout to the most uninhibited race prejudice. The editorial columns of the *Bulletin*

> 'fairly bristled with such emotionally charged words as "niggers", "Chows", "Japs", "mongrelised races".... More potent still were the cartoons that portrayed the coloured man as a grinning caricature of humanity...'.[1]

And the Brisbane *Worker,* although claiming to be striving for a classless society, regularly carried similar cartoons as well as vitriolic verses insulting to non-Whites.

Causes of colour prejudice in South Africa

The ferocity of proletarian colour antagonism, as manifested in the writer's own country, South Africa, has interested and puzzled him for four decades. Because the very human weaknesses involved are so relevant to the migration difficulties of the present era, the three following paragraphs are devoted to a consideration of the sources of this ferocity.

The clue to the intense bitterness of racial prejudice in South Africa is, we suggest, to be found chiefly in the fact that, as long as each generation can remember, non-Whites have been confined to the lowest-paid kind of work. This occurred initially through custom but was perpetuated mainly through the union-enforced principle of 'the rate for the job', which always bears unfavourably and unfairly on 'non-preferred' or less well-equipped persons, especially when reinforced by legislation.[2] It is the situation created by the denial to such persons of access to the wage bargaining table which, through perpetuating the economic inferiority of non-Whites, has kept alive a fear that is not without some justification. The privileged Whites feel intuitively that equality of opportunity would give rise to a particularly disastrous intensity of competition.

The element of reality in the fear derives from a realisation that most non-white races multiply rapidly in comparison with most

---

1 *Ibid.,* p. 43.

2 Particularly the *Industrial Conciliation Act* (1942) and the *Wage Act* (1925). 'Job reservations' are more obvious but *less important* colour bars in practice (less important, except for the barriers enforced through the Mines and Works Acts, 1911 and 1926, which exclude non-Whites from skilled or responsible work in the mines and associated industries). 'Job reservations' are less permanent causes of racial and class injustice because *they* are not approved by their victims.

white races.[1] But the writer has diagnosed the horror of reduced status as the prime factor. It is the thought that competition may close the gap between the economic condition of Whites and non-Whites which has caused the white proletariat in South Africa to reject the principle of preserving 'civilised standards' yet permitting a 'levelling-up' process. It is easy to perceive in South Africa how the racial stratification of the wage-earning structure (which persists for the reasons noticed in the preceding paragraph) has continuously frustrated any chance of peaceful and early solution of the race problem.

Ever since a trusting or cynical British Liberal Party sponsored the South Africa Act, renouncing thereby almost all British responsibilities towards non-Whites in the new Union of South Africa (1910),[2] the easiest way to the maintenance or acquisition of political power in that country has been to exploit the fears which are inevitable when the colour-blind free market is threatening to dissolve privileges. A policy which had aimed at preventing a catastrophically sudden dissolution of established expectations, yet permitting gradual access to the more productive and well-paid occupations for the different non-white groups, would have had much to be said for it under 'classic liberal' ideals. The established expectations of white workers who, as individuals, could not be held responsible for the inherited privileges to which they had adjusted their lives, were capable of recognition in policy. White artisans could have been insulated against any intolerable *absolute* decline in material well-being, although not against any decline in *relative status*. But under the conditions created, it was always difficult for politicians to forego the votes to be won by pandering to the white proletariat's determination to preserve *relative* standards and status.

Parallels in the USA

This much may be said in defence of the South African politicians: their chief critics in the world, however different the critics' ideals, have acquiesced in virtually the same policy. For instance, in the United States after the First World War, free market forces were slowly but relentlessly eroding time-honoured barriers to equality of opportunity. A growing proportion of Negroes, acquiring property

---

[1] This is equally true, however, of the relatively poor everywhere, although racial traditions and religious principles do have an influence.

[2] The South Africa Act contained 'entrenched clauses' which, it was believed, would protect the voting rights of non-Whites in the Cape and Natal. Subsequent British legislation made it possible for the South African Government, *via* the subterfuge of packing the Senate, to tear up these entrenchments.

and self-respect, were thinking of themselves as good Americans, proud of their country and their flag. The conspicuous acceptance of non-Whites as social equals—particularly among children and students—and the evasion of market obstacles were together laying foundations for the removal of surviving restraints on civil rights. There was rearguard action by the KKK and a 'lunatic fringe'. But opposition of that kind would soon have lost its force if pre-1930 economic freedom had been preserved.

Unfortunately, as rapidly as custom-based barriers to opportunities for non-Whites were being demolished, new ones were erected in the form of the Walsh-Healy Act, the Wagner Act and the Fair Labor Standards Act. This legislation created colour bars similar to those of the South African 'civilised labour' or *'apartheid'* policies. Intentions were somewhat different, but the consequences have been of the same type (although not quite as difficult to remedy). In the circumstances produced, everything favoured those politicians, black or white, who saw profit in the exacerbation of colour, racial and class resentments among the Blacks. Far-seeing Negroes who perceived what was happening were increasingly condemned to silence through fear of appearing as traitors to their people's cause or through fear of violence.[1] For most Negro leaders so thirsted for early power that they were tempted to play on the jealousies and suspicions of their fellows, instead of drawing attention to the almost unprecedented idealism, goodwill and charity of the majority of middle-class and upper-class white Americans.

The purpose of this discussion has not been to blame or condemn South African or US politicians but to illustrate the kind of difficulties which the 'White Australia' policy avoided. Humanitarians must surely praise the prescience of those Australian leaders at the turn of the century who, although they deplored the racism of the 'Labour' press and the 'Labour' politicians, threw their weight into a determination to maintain, as far as possible, a racially homogeneous Australia.

V. CONCLUSION: HARNESSING THE MARKET TO LIBERAL IDEALS

The notion of one citizenship for all races within the Commonwealth expressed a noble ideal. But *it cannot be an acceptable ideal* until

---

[1] One vital difference in South Africa is that African or other political trouble-makers have been effectively suppressed, unfortunately by ruthless methods which have (unnecessarily in the writer's judgement) entailed suspension of the rule of law. Another vital difference is that most Africans still share in the virtues of tribal culture, whereas American Negroes are purely American, even those who resent being reminded of it.

the peoples of the world have been taught to use the market to curb the cupidity of man, to harness the sister virtues of thrift and generosity for the good of humanity, and to conquer the curse of unbridled breeding. The pricing anarchy created when wage-rates are determined under political motivations and the strike-threat leaves conditions which are incompatible with the peaceful integration of cultures.

The tragedy is that a mingling of traditions through human migrations *could* bring richness of experience and living everywhere. Mankind has everything to gain from the cross-fertilisation of ideas and ways of life. Yet the stimuli of contacts between civilisations and cultures must be renounced until such clashes of economic interest as occur can be resolved impersonally through the free market.[1]

Immigrants with rare skills, knowledge of developing techniques and new ideas appear always to have brought great materials benefits to the countries of their choice. Emigré victims of religious intolerance in the 17th and 18th centuries found freedom and prosperity in the lands to which they fled, but the nations which welcomed them gained more than proportionally. And in our age Jewish refugees brought formidable advantages to many countries through their technological 'know how', managerial expertise, enterprise and entrepreneurial experience in new spheres. But these benefits also appear to be becoming increasingly difficult to win if over-population is to be avoided. For such adverse effects of population growth upon per capita income as are observable in the present seem to be traceable everywhere to the disco-ordinative consequences of *dirigiste* policy. In these circumstances, controls designed to achieve the benefits of immigration without the burden of population on output having to be shouldered, must almost inevitably *appear* to discriminate on class or racial grounds. The dilemma cannot be avoided.

---

[1] Collective restraints may have a role in the softening of adjustment pains.

3. THE MOVEMENT OF HUMAN CAPITAL

SUDHA SHENOY

THE AUTHOR

Sudha R. Shenoy was born on 12 September, 1943, and educated at
Mount Carmel Convent School and St. Xavier's College, Ahmedabad,
India, the London School of Economics, 1963-66, the University of
Virginia, 1967-68, and the School of Oriental and African Studies,
University of London, 1968-69. She is a B.A. (Hons.), Economics
and Politics, Gujarat University, 1963, B. Sc. (Econ.), University of
London, 1966, and M.A. (Area Studies), in the Economics and History
of South Asia, University of London, 1969. She is presently Economic
Research Officer at the Commonwealth Secretariat.

Her publications include 'The Sources of Monopoly', *New Individual-
ist Review,* Spring 1966; 'Pricing for Refuse Removal', in *Essays in
the Theory and Practice of Pricing,* Readings in Political Economy 3,
IEA, 1967; and *Underdevelopment and Economic Growth,* Key Book 10,
Longmans for the IEA, 1970.

1. INTRODUCTION

The 'brain drain'[1]—so-called—from the under-developed to the developed areas, and especially to the United States, has become a subject of frequent comment, both political and journalistic,[2] as well as an issue of some controversy among economists.[3] The out-

---

[1] I deal here with the movement of human capital *per se,* i.e., of those individuals possessing scientific, technical, medical or other academic qualifications, the acquisition of which requires a fair amount of investment (in terms of direct expenditure and income foregone), in contrast with the movement of skilled labour.

[2] Sen. Walter Mondale, 'The Brain Drain from Developing Countries', *Congressional Record,* Vol. 112, 31 August, 1965, pp. 20589-20593; 'Migration of Talented Professional People to the U.S.A.', *ibid.,* 9 September, 1966, pp. 21262-21274; 'How Poor Nations Give to the Rich', *Saturday Review,* 11 March, 1967; Ian Ball, 'Brain Drain to U.S. Valued at $4,000 million', *Daily Telegraph,* 7 November, 1966; R. K. Shrivastava, 'The Brain Drain', *Hindusthan Times,* 23 February 1966; K. Bhaskara Rao, 'India's Brain-Drain: Flight of Talent', *Indian Express,* 25 and 26 April, 1965; Lord Hailsham, 'Emigration of Scientists from the United Kingdom', House of Lords *Hansard,* Vol. 247, No. 47, 27 February, 1963, cols. 92-95, 181-182. The foregoing is a random selection from a large number of similar items.

[3] The first shot was fired by Brinley Thomas, 'Trends in the International Migration of Skilled Manpower', *International Migration,* July-September 1961. Then came H. G. Johnson, 'The Economics of the 'Brain Drain': The Canadian Case', *Minerva,* Spring 1965, followed in succession by H. G. Grubel and A. D. Scott, 'The International Flow of Human Capital', *American Economic Review,* May 1966 (with comments by Burton A. Weisbrod and H. G. Johnson); Brinley Thomas, 'The International Circulation of Human Capital', *Minerva,* Summer 1967 (followed by letters from H. G. Johnson and A. D. Scott in *Minerva,* Autumn 1967, with a reply by Brinley Thomas in *Minerva,* Spring 1968); H. G. Johnson, 'An 'Internationalist' Model', Don Patinkin, 'A 'Nationalist' Model', and K. E. Boulding, 'The 'National' Importance of Human Capital', in Walter Adams (ed.), *The Brain Drain* (London and New York, Macmillan, 1968); H. G. Grubel, 'The Reduction of the Brain Drain; Problems and Policies', *Minerva,* Summer 1968, followed by a

flow of technically-qualified individuals from under-developed areas is part of a wider circulation of human capital,[1] among the developed countries. The exact dimensions of this phenomenon are not as yet known: while the inflows into the United States are better charted than others, flows elsewhere have not yet been fully explored.

2. THE EXTENT OF THE 'DRAIN'

The United States has been increasingly attracting qualified people, both from the developed and the under-developed worlds (Table 1).[2]

TABLE 1. Immigration of Scientists, Engineers and Physicians into the US, 1956-67

	Total	Index	Developed Countries	%	Developing Countries	%
1956	5313	100.0	3604	67.1	1769	32.9
1962	5956	110.8	3573	60.0	2383	40.0
1963	7896	147.0	4534	57.4	3362	42.6
1964	7810	145.4	4607	59.0	3202	41.0
1965	7198	134.0	4548	63.2	2650	36.8
1966	9534	177.4	5144	54.0	4390	46.0
1967	15272	284.2	7359	48.2	7913	51.8

Source: *The Brain Drain of Scientists, Engineers and Physicians from the Developing Countries into the United States,* Hearings before a Subcommittee of the Committee on Government Operations, House of Representatives (Washington, D.C.: US Government Printing Office, 1968), Tables 1 and 2.

---

letter from Brinley Thomas, in *Minerva,* Autumn-Winter 1968-69. Also S. Kannappan, 'The Brain Drain and Developing Countries', *International Labour Review,* July 1968; S. Watanabe, 'The Brain Drain from Developing to Developed Countries', *ibid.,* April 1969; and Albert E. Gollin (ed.), *The International Migration of Talent and Skills,* proceedings of a Workshop and Conference sponsored by the Council on International Educational and Cultural Affairs, U.S. Government (Washington D.C., 1966).

[1] Cf. Brinley Thomas' article in *Minerva* (footnote 3, page 47).

[2] The addition of dentists, nurses and social scientists would raise these totals substantially, as can be seen from the Table opposite.

Table 2 further analyses the part played by developing countries in this influx of skilled manpower.

With the passage of the new Immigration Act of 1965, which abolished racial quotas, but introduced quotas based on skills,[1] the door has opened wider for the emigration to the U.S. of over-developed people from under-developed countries.[2]

Canada and Australia are the other known magnets for the brainy, mainly, however, from other developed areas. Between 1950 and 1963, Canada received an average of 7,790 professional immigrants every year (including 1,230 from the U.S.),[3] while Australia 'imported' an annual average of 5,320 professional and technical workers, between 1949 and 1966.[4] Canada's close proximity to the U.S., however, has meant a heavy outflow as well: between 1950 and 1963, an annual average of 4,681 professionals emigrated over the border. Of these, 3,041 were Canadian-born.[5]

Immigration of Scientists, Engineers and Medical Personnel into the United States, 1962-66

	1962	*1963*	*1964*	*1965*	*1966*
From developed countries	6,651	8,138	8,171	8,145	7,909
From under-developed countries	3,197	4,344	4,152	3,604	5,540
Total	9,848	12,482	12,323	11,749	13,449

Source: US House of Representatives, Committee on Government Operations, *The Brain Drain Into the United States of Scientists, Engineers and Physicians* (Washington, D.C., 1967), Appendix A, Tables I-V.

[1] Cf. the discussion in Brinley Thomas, 'From the other Side: A European View', *Annals of the American Academy of Political and Social Science,* September 1966 (Issue entitled 'The New Immigration').

[2] The phrase has been attributed to Professor Abdus Salam, F.R.S. An Indian travel agency has already started advertising aimed at intending immigrants to the USA, Canada and Australia. (*The Statesman,* Calcutta, 2 June, 1969.)

[3] Louis Parai, *Immigration and Emigration of Professional and Skilled Manpower During the Post War Period,* Special Study No. 1, Economic Council of Canada (Ottawa: The Queen's Printer, 1965), p. 33.

[4] *Australian Immigration: Consolidated Statistics* (Canberra: Department of Immigration, 1966), as cited in Brinley Thomas' article in *Minerva.*

[5] Parai, *op. cit.*

TABLE 2. Immigration of Scientists, Engineers and Physicians from Developing Areas into the US, 1956–67

	Scientists		Engineers		Physicians	
	Total (all countries)	*% from Developing Areas*	*Total (all countries)*	*% from Developing Areas*	*Total (all countries)*	*% from Developing Areas*
1956	1022	34.9	2804	25.4	1547	45.2
1962	1104	26.9	2940	33.5	1912	57.6
1963	1612	34.9	4014	40.9	2270	51.0
1964	1676	32.6	3725	36.8	2409	53.3
1965	1549	27.0	3455	30.4	2194	53.8
1966	1852	41.2	4921	40.9	2761	58.5
1967	2893	50.9	8822	47.9	3557	62.2

Source: As for Table 1: Tables 1 and 3.

Another country with a heavy two-way traffic in skills is the UK. While the *out*flow has been approximately equally divided between North America and other countries, the *in*flow has come mainly from the latter (Table 3).

An average of 500 doctors a year *left* Britain between 1954 and 1963.[1] The *in*flow of doctors, mainly for short-term hospital posts, is indicated by the rising percentage of junior hospital staff (in England and Wales) who were born outside the British Isles: from 39 per cent in 1961, this figure rose to 44 per cent three years later, when 4,300 junior doctors came from overseas.[2] During the eighteen-month period ending 30 June 1969, a total of 1,555 doctors from the Commonwealth entered the country.[3] While these doctors are by no means part of the 'brain-drain', they provide some measure of British short-term imports of medical skills.

On the side of the under-developed countries, the available data are uncertain. According to some sources, about 11,125 Indians with technical, medical and scientific qualifications were resident abroad in 1966.[4] Other guesses place the figure at around 20,000.[5] Since these figures represent an approximation to the stock abroad up to that year, it seems clear that the substantial majority were in countries *other* than the U.S: total skilled immigration into that country, between 1956 and 1967, came to 3,105.[6] There are only very fragmentary indications of other flows. The number of Greeks abroad, with scientific and professional qualifications, equalled 14.3 per cent of all such Greek graduates in the period 1961-1965.[7] The Egyptian government reportedly has begun encouraging the emigration of

---

1   J. R. Seale, 'Medical Emigration: A Study in the Inadequacy of Official Statistics', in *Lessons From Central Forecasting*, Eaton Paper 6, Institute of Economic Affairs, 1965.

2   Office of Health Economics, *Medical Manpower*, London, 1966, Table D, p. 17.

3   Ministry of Health.

4   M. Blaug, P. R. G. Layard, M. Woodhall, *The Causes of Educated Unemployment in India* (forthcoming), Ch.6, and S. P. Awasthi, 'An experiment in voluntary repatriation of high-level technical manpower: the Scientists' Pool,' *Economic Weekly*, 18 September, 1965.

5   K. Ray, 'Utilising India's Absentee Manpower', *The Statesman* (Calcutta), 1 July, 1967.

6   Blaug, Layard and Woodhall, *op. cit.*

7   G. Coutsoumaris, 'Greece', in W. Adams (ed.), *op. cit.*, p. 170.

TABLE 3. Flow of Engineers, Scientists and Technologists between the UK and the Rest of the World, 1961-66

	Outflow			Inflow		
	All countries	*North America*	*Other countries*	*All countries*	*North America*	*Other countries*
1961	3220	1285	1935	3215	835	2380
1962	3510	1440	2070	3170	870	2300
1963	3965	1665	2300	2535	760	1775
1964	4745	1970	2775	3170	865	2305
1965	5065	2355	2710	3290	905	2385
1966	6215	3105	3110	3520	940	2580

Source: Committee on Manpower Resources for Science and Technology, *The Brain Drain*, Report of a Working Group (HMSO, 1967), Appendix D, Tables 1 and 2. Figures underlined are estimates from incomplete data; orders of magnitude.

educated Egyptians to the U.S., Canada, and Western Europe.[1] Of the 5,000 Argentinian engineers said to be working abroad in 1966,[2] some 984 are in the U.S., others may be in Venezuela and Brazil.[3] Greek, Turkish, and Yugoslav engineers emigrate to other parts of Europe.[4] Norwegian and Swiss engineers have joined their confreres abroad.[5] Sweden both imports and exports graduates.[6] Concern has been expressed over the number of talented Iranis,[7] Israelis,[8] Chileans,[9] Peruvians[10] and Argentinians[11] working abroad, especially in the U.S.[12]

1   Raymond H. Anderson in *The Times of India* (Bombay), 30 June, 1969, from the *New York Times* News Service.

2   S. Dedijer, 'Migration of Scientists: A World Wide Phenomenon and Problem', *Nature*, 7 March, 1964.

3   Enrique Oteiza, 'Emigration of engineers from Argentina: a case of Latin American brain drain', *International Labour Review*, December 1965.

4   S. Dedijer, *op. cit.*

5   S. Dedijer, *op. cit.;* Brinley Thomas' article in *Minerva*.

6   S. Dedijer, *op. cit.*, G. Friborg, 'Migration av akademiker till och fran Sverige', *Tchnisk Vetenskaplig Forskning*, Stockholm, 1965.

7   Habib Naficy, *The Brain Drain: The Case of Iranian non-returnees*, Report to the Annual Conference of the Society for International Development, New York, 1966.

8   Burton M. Halpern, 'New Exodus: Israel's Talent Drain', *The Nation*, 10 May, 1965; 'Israel Issues Appeal for Skilled Workers', *New York Post*, 23 July, 1965.

9   O. S. Gutierrez and P. J. Riquelme, 'The Emigration of High-Level Skilled Chilean Human Resources to the United States', *Ciencia Interamericana*, March-April 1965.

10   Robert Myers, 'The Migration of Human Resources and Foreign Student Non-return, with Special Reference to Peru', Dissertation proposal, Comparative Education Centre, University of Chicago, January, 1966.

11   Oteiza, *op. cit.*, Morris A. Horowitz, 'High level manpower in the Economic Development of Argentina', in F. Harbison and C. A. Myers (eds.), *Manpower and Education*, McGraw-Hill, New York, 1965.

12   Pan-American Health Organization, *Migration of Health Personnel, Scientists and Engineers from Latin America*, Washington, D. C., 1966.

These international flows of human capital are fed from a second source: the non-returning student. Here, too, the U.S. figures are the best available. During 1967, almost half of all students from developing countries elected to remain (Table 4).

TABLE 4. Students Adjusting to Immigrant Status in US, 1967

	(A) Total	(B) Adjusting Status from Student to Immigrant	(C) B as % of A
Total	15, 272	3648	23. 9
Developed Countries	7, 359	278	3. 8
Developing Countries	7, 913	3370	42. 6
Taiwan	1, 321	1137	86. 1
India	1, 425	1074	75. 4
Korea	269	193	71. 7
Iran	286	144	50. 3
Israel	206	71	34. 5

Source: As for Table 1: Table 4.

The number of scientists, engineers, and medical personnel emigrating to the U.S. in 1966-7 from the developing countries, came to 10, 250. In the case of Taiwan and India, the number of immigrants (1, 407 and 1, 485 respectively) approximately equalled the number of non-returning students.[1]

The percentages of Ph.D. recipients who remained in the U.S. were somewhat higher than the overall average, according to a survey by the National Academy of Science, covering some 84 per cent of all foreign Ph.D. students (Table 5).

The contribution of this channel to the flow of skills into *other* areas is in need of investigation. In 1963, there were over 25, 000 foreign students in West German universities;[2] 16, 915 overseas students

---

[1] *The Brain Drain of Scientists, Engineers and Physicians from the Developing Countries Into the United States,* Hearings before a Subcommittee of the Committee on Government Operations, U.S. House of Representatives (Washington, D.C., 1968), Appendix.

[2] Prodosh Aich, 'Asian and African Students in West German Universities', *Minerva,* Summer 1963.

TABLE 5. Foreign Ph.D. Recipients Returning or Remaining in US, 1964-66

Region of first degree	Returning	%	Remaining in US	%
Australasia	174	59	100	34
East Asia	200	24	571	68
West Asia	586	36	741	45
Africa	79	75	21	20
Europe	212	28	418	55
South America	84	64	44	33
North and Central America	520	57	343	38

Source: As for Table 1: p. 16.

were taking full-time courses in British universities in 1966-67;[1] Canada had 11,284 foreign students in 1965-66;[2] the numbers for Australia and New Zealand were 5,007 and 1,147 respectively, in 1966.[3] The numbers of those remaining, or being 'drained' elsewhere is unknown. From the side of the developing countries (or those exporting talent), a Cento Science Survey Mission estimated in 1963 that some 50 per cent of all Turkish, Irani and Pakistani students reading for scientific degrees in foreign universities failed to return.[4] Similarly, African and Vietnamese students in France are 'drained off'.[5] According to the Indian Education Commission, there were 15,400 Indian students and trainees abroad in 1964.[6] A total of 8,800 Greek students (almost a quarter of all Greek university students) were studying abroad in 1964.[7]

---

[1] *Annual Abstract of Statistics,* 1968, Table 119.

[2] *Commonwealth Universities' Yearbook,* 1967-68, p. 1007.

[3] *Ibid.,* p. 28.

[4] *Report of the Cento Science Survey Mission,* 1963, pp. 11-12.

[5] J. P. N'Diaye, *Enquetes sur les etudiants noirs en France,* Paris, 1962; 'Les etudiants Africains en France', *Le Monde,* 2 July, 1964; G. Emerson, 'Vietnamese trained in Paris Refuse to Go Home', *New York Times,* 13 March, 1966.

[6] Government of India, Education Commission, *Report,* 1965, p. 280n.

[7] George V. Haniotis, 'An Exercise in Voluntary Repatriation in Greece', *OECD Observer,* August 1964.

3. RETURN FLOWS

Return flows have also not been charted. 5,000 Indians were estimated to have returned to the country by 1966.[1] But the numbers
leaving for a *second* time is not known, although there is some slight
evidence for this phenomenon.[2] 38,800 of the 44,800 professional
and technical migrants who left Puerto Rico between 1957 and 1960
are estimated to have returned.[3] Between 1960 and 1964, while
3,531 professional and technical workers left Argentina for the U.S.,
3,858 such individuals entered Argentina from other countries.[4]

The value of the human capital involved in these international flows
is conjectural, at best. The only estimates are for the United States
and Canada. Grubel and Scott[5] valued the replacement costs, in U.S.
terms, of the inflow of scientists and engineers, for the period
1949-61, at $1,055 million.[6] The calculations made by Louis Parai[7]
suggests that skills worth approximately $170 million were imported
into Canada during the decade 1953-63, after adjusting for outflows
to the U.S., the average annual inflow being $17 million. This last
came to about 3.8 per cent of current university expenditure in
Canada in 1965-66.

The inflow of skills into the U.S. in 1963-64, equalled 3 per cent of
all U.S. first degrees in the natural sciences; 11 per cent of the first
degrees in engineering; and 29 per cent of all M.D.'s.[8] One fourth
of all interns, and one third of all residents in American hospitals,
are from overseas.[9] The total immigration of engineers, in the nine

---

[1] Blaug, Layard, and Woodhall, *op. cit.*

[2] Blaug, Layard, and Woodhall, *op. cit;* S. P. Awasthi, *op. cit.* Also
     'The Plight of a Specialist' by A Young Engineer, *Swarajya*
     (Madras), 15 April, 1967.

[3] W. H. Knowles, 'Manpower and education in Puerto Rico', in
     Harbison and Myers (eds.), *op. cit.*

[4] Pan American Health Organisation, *op. cit.,* p. 10, Table 3.

[5] H. G. Grubel and A. D. Scott, 'The Immigration of Scientists and
     Engineers to the United States, 1949-61', *Journal of Political
     Economy,* August 1966.

[6] Cf. too the letter from J. Douglas Muir in *Minerva,* Spring 1969.

[7] Parai, *op. cit.,* pp. 79-83.

[8] Thomas J. Mills, 'Scientific Personnel and the Professions',
     Annals of the American Academy, etc., *op. cit.*

[9] Charles V. Kidd, Written evidence, in *The Brain Drain....* etc.,
     op. cit.

years to 1965, equalled the total number of U.S. engineering graduates in 1965.[1] This inflow is said to offset the outflow of U.S. aid,
especially to developing areas.[2]

On the side of the exporting countries, we have already seen that
there are a fair number of Greek graduates abroad.[3] The number
of Argentinian engineers abroad may be of the order of 8 per cent of
the country's engineering graduates in the decade 1951-61.[4] 23 per
cent of all Norwegian engineering graduates in the years 1946-60
emigrated, as did 5 per cent of all German science graduates.[5] 22.4
per cent of Swiss graduate engineers, and 21.8 per cent of Dutch
engineers, emigrated to the U.S. in the period 1956-61.[6] Between 1961
and 1965, the number of physicians migrating from Central America
to the U.S. equalled 22 per cent of all medical graduates in these
countries.[7] The total number of Indian scientists, engineers and
doctors working abroad has been estimated to equal about 3 per cent
of the stock in India, and 30 per cent of the annual output in 1965.[8]

4.   ECONOMIC EFFECTS AND REMEDIES

Data regarding the precise magnitudes and directions of the international flow of skills are, as we have seen, uncertain at best. Nevertheless, it has been forcefully argued[9] that the 'brain drain' im-
pinges heavily on the under-developed areas in particular. The

---

[1]   Thomas J. Mills, *op. cit.*

[2]   For instance, James A. Perkins, 'Foreign Aid and the Brain
Drain', *Foreign Affairs,* July, 1966. Cf. also the letter by J.
Douglas Muir in *Minerva,* Spring 1969.

[3]   Above, pages 54-55.

[4]   Oteiza, *op. cit.*

[5]   S. Dedijer, *op. cit.*; Brinley Thomas' article in *Minerva*.

[6]   Brinley Thomas' article in *Minerva*.

[7]   Pan American Health Organization, *op. cit.*, p. 18.

[8]   Blaug, Layard, Woodhall, *op. cit.*

[9]   Articles and letters by Brinley Thomas, cited in fn. 3, pp. 47-48; S.
Watanabe, *op. cit.*, Don Patinkin, *op. cit.*, K. E. Boulding, *op. cit.*,
Thomas J. Mills, *op. cit.*, Charles V. Kidd, *op. cit.*, and *idem*, 'The
Loss of Scientists From Less to More Developed Countries' in
Vol. IX of *U.S. Papers Prepared for the U.N. Conference on the
Application of Science and Technology for the Benefit of the Less
Developed Areas* (Washington D.C., 1963); James A. Perkins, *op.
cit.*, E. Oteiza, *op. cit.* Also see *The Brain Drain.....* etc., *op. cit.*

major adverse effect said to result from the unhampered movement of skilled personnel across international frontiers, is that these areas are deprived thereby of the possibility of developing an indigenous body of scientific and technological knowledge—i.e., there is a loss of 'spillover' effects. Development may be held up by the absence of crucial human inputs at a critical stage of the economy's forward movement.

On the basis of this analysis, various measures have been advocated for stemming the 'brain drain', and/or for retaining or attracting many who might otherwise emigrate.[1] While only one writer, an Indian,[2] has recommended a ban on emigration, other suggestions have included imposing more stringent conditions for immigration into the U.S., the establishment of an international fund to provide compensation to countries 'losing' skilled personnel, and the imposition of an emigrants' tax.[3] On the side of the under-developed countries, it has been suggested that research institutions should be set up, with suitable working conditions for scientists and technologists; that these two groups should be closely associated with high level policy-making; that an adequate supply of scientific books, journals, and instruments be made available; and that travelling fellowships be provided to overcome scientific isolation. Higher remuneration has also been recommended.[4]

Measures aimed specifically at student 'drainees'[5] include closer supervision of their training abroad; a more careful selection of their course of studies; and the tailoring of special courses to fit their needs. It has also been suggested that only the more mature students who have already established career and family ties in their home countries, be allowed to go abroad.

5. ECONOMIC IMPLICATIONS

This analysis, as well as the measures mentioned above, raises a number of issues. In the first place, the *lack* of suitable research

---

[1] For instance, Charles V. Kidd, *op. cit.*

[2] V. M. Dandekar, 'India', in W. Adams, *op. cit.*

[3] Cf. S. Watanabe, *op. cit.*

[4] *International Migration of Talent From and To the Less Developed Countries*, Report of a Conference at Ditchley Park, 16-19 February, 1968.

[5] For example, the oral and written evidence by the Rev. W. J. Gibbons, S. J., Dr. John C. Shearer, Dr. William C. Thiesenhusen, and Dr. Charles V. Kidd in *The Brain Drain...* etc., *op. cit.*

institutions implies the opposite of unsatisfied demand for high- or even medium-level scientific and technological skills. While exact figures are not available, there is some evidence for the existence of a large volume of educated unemployment in under-developed areas. The Indian case, for instance, is the subject of a forthcoming study.[1] According to a review by the Government of India's Directorate General of Employment and Training, there was a 31.3 per cent increase in the number of graduates seeking employment in 1967-68, over the previous year, but the number of vacancies fell by 13.6 per cent.[2] Total educated unemployment is conjectured to be 1.5 million[3] in 1968. The figure of 90,000 unemployed engineers has been quoted in the Indian press.[4] More dramatically, the All-India Youth Federation and the All-India Students' Federation sponsored a mass fast in May 1969 in New Delhi, to draw the attention of Parliament to the problem of educated unemployment.[5] One official attempt to repatriate Indian scientists was relatively unsuccessful: over 30 per cent of those repatriated were still unemployed at the end of the first year; at the end of the second year, this percentage had risen to 40.[6]

There are reportedly 35,000 unemployed graduates in the Phillipines; while graduates of the University of Khartum besieged the government for jobs.[7] Only 1,200 out of 23,000 Korean graduates had jobs in 1966.[8]

As for proposals to further restrict students' choice of subjects, this is already done in many under-developed areas by exchange control. Thus in India, in order to 'conserve' foreign exchange, students are permitted to go abroad only for scientific, technical and medical courses not available at home, and only *after* the completion of a first degree. Paradoxically, students may *then* find that their

---

1   Blaug, Layard, Woodhall, *op. cit.*

2   *The Statesman* (Calcutta), 28 May, 1969.

3   S. K. Haldar, 'How Not to Tackle the Problem of Educated Unemployed', *The Statesman* (Calcutta), 10 July, 1969.

4   *Indian Express* (Bombay), 26 June, 1969. The latest estimates (from the Indian Institute of Engineers and the Institute of Applied Manpower Research) place it at about 55,000. (*Financial Express* (Bombay), 12 January, 1970; *Times of India* (Bombay), 18 March, 1970.)

5   *Indian Express* (Bombay), 15 May, 1969.

6   S. P. Awasthi, *op. cit.*

7   Dr. G. Halsey Hunt, *The Brain Drain. . . . .* etc., *op. cit.*

8   G. Emerson in the *New York Times*, 27 February, 1966.

specialisms are unsuited to the Indian context. In this case, as in so many others, government policy has had an opposite effect to the one intended. Many scholarships, or other forms of assistance, may similarly be linked to specified subjects, or may be granted on condition of a certain period of service in developing areas. Thus, those who received Indian government assistance are required to return to India, and, in the case of teachers, to remain for three years in government service.[1]

6. UNDERPRICING THE COSTS OF EDUCATION

It is true that in many countries government policy underprices the exchange purchased to finance foreign study; policy may also make domestic education available at nominal fees or at less than full cost. This subsidy, it is suggested,[2] may be a partial measure of the 'loss' from the 'brain drain'. However, there is nothing inevitable about such institutional arrangements: from the recipients' viewpoint, these subsidies are windfall gains—and policy could be suitably altered so as to make both exchange and education available at market prices.

7. HUMAN AND PHYSICAL CAPITAL

Interregional movements of this kind, *within* international boundaries, seldom arouse attention—it is only movements *across* such frontiers which are the objects of concern. We may ask in this connection whether the economic 'problems' of Scotland and Appalachia (such as they are) would be lessened or resolved by the 'repatriation' of talented individuals? Do these areas really suffer from the lack of human inputs, from the lack of an indigenous body of locally-applicable scientific and technological 'know-how'? Would they 'benefit' if Appalachian or Scottish students were forbidden to study subjects with no direct application in these areas?

In other words, the *complementarity* of human and physical capital formation is crucial: investment in some types of human capital may be 'appropriate' only in conjunction with a specific level of *physical* capital formation. The under-developed areas lack not only science and technology, and the sort of medical care found only in developed areas, but also simple food, shelter and clothing. This situation is the outcome of a very low level of *physical* capital formation; the

---

[1] Government of India, Ministry of Education, *Scholarships for Studies Abroad* (1960 edn.), p. 30.

[2] S. Watanabe, *op. cit.*

creation or retention of high-level *human* capital can hardly be said to provide a substitute. This point is relevant, especially, to the consideration of 'spillover' effects. The invention of the electric light bulb has not yet brought illumination to the vast mass of the people living in poor countries; a substantial amount of physical capital is required before this can happen.[1] Additional research institutions may not result in the production of the physical capital necessary to *apply* technological advances on a mass scale.

However, *medical* emigration is said to be different. It has been stated[2] that such migration reduces the availability of medical care in under-developed areas; its control has therefore been suggested in the interests of their inhabitants. But such medical care is generally produced at capital costs well beyond the reach of the masses in the under-developed areas; people who live in mud huts, on the verge of subsistence, can scarcely be said to be in a position to demand the sort of medical care within the reach of e.g., many Americans. (Those who have no bread cannot, of course, eat cake.) Reducing the inflow of overseas doctors into the American economy would, however, raise returns to *American* doctors,[3] while reducing (potential) returns to doctors who might otherwise have immigrated. In many instances, these doctors come from families who live at standards far below those found in Appalachia; they represent, as it were, the accumulated savings of a number of relatively poor people, who would now be deprived of the opportunity of obtaining substantially higher returns on their investment.

In under-developed areas, education is very largely paid for directly out of parental and/or relatives' incomes. Given the relatively low level of real incomes in these areas, the education of an individual involves substantial sacrifices in terms of both current and potential incomes foregone. Restricting the mobility of the human capital thus formed means that these savers are debarred from obtaining the highest potential returns on their private venture investment.

The problem, in other words, is one of selecting that 'mix' of investment in both human and physical capital, which will maximise returns to *all* forms of labour. Consider once more the case of Scotland. Given the current level of physical capital formation in Scotland, would the repatriation of Scottish graduates result in an increase in returns to *all* Scotsmen (with or without 'spillover'

---

1 I am indebted to Professor B.R. Shenoy for this observation.

2 E.g., S. Kannappan, *op. cit.*

3 I am indebted for this observation to Mr Hamish Gray. Reducing inflows of other skills would similarly raise returns to the American suppliers of these talents.

effects)? Alternatively, if more Scotsmen were kept at 'home', with a lesser amount of human capital invested in them, and the savings invested in *physical* capital instead, would *this* result in higher returns all round?

South India is another case in point. For some three generations now, South Indians have emigrated from their chiefly rice-growing agricultural 'home' regions to other parts of India, as officials, office workers, clerks, nurses, and school and university teachers. They represent a considerable volume of human capital exported from this part of India to other areas. Given the current level of physical capital in the South, it does not seem obvious that repatriation would be the best method of raising the aggregate incomes of all South Indians; if, on the other hand, South Indian decision-makers had selected a capital 'mix' with relatively more physical investment (on the four- or five-acre rice-growing farms which largely make up the South Indian economy) and relatively less human investment, one may doubt that it would have raised the aggregate earnings of *all* South Indians.[1]

This does not imply, of course, that the level of physical capital ought not or cannot be raised very substantially. But reducing the returns to *human* investment does not seem to be the most appropriate method of achieving this objective.[2]

8. STUDENT NON-RETURNEES

First, the larger proportion of students going overseas *do* return; this substantial *reverse* flow of human capital has not received full consideration in the discussions of the 'brain drain'. Secondly, the capital investment in these students is made out of the resources of the area in which the education is received: where the student returns 'home', there is a capital inflow into the receiving country, but if the student *fails* to return, this 'non-return' is hardly the equivalent of a positive capital transfer *out* of his 'home' country. This is even clearer where the education is financed out of scholarships, or employment, in the educating country.

The very concepts of a 'brain drain', and a 'national loss' from the 'flight' (escape?) of talented people, carry with them the implication that the individuals involved are a national resource—nationalised

---

[1] What about the alternative of physical investment in export industries? The same argument would apply: it is questionable whether such an investment 'mix' would raise the total earnings of *all* the individuals involved.

[2] S. Watanabe, *op. cit.*

serfs, akin to the talented Greek slaves bought by Romans to manage their estates and educate their children. Proposals to reimburse the 'losing' countries point up this runaway slave analogy even more clearly. But reduction of world poverty implies that individuals and families which were formerly 'poor' now obtain higher real incomes: if to achieve this involves movement across international frontiers (rather than interregional boundaries), the end-result is still the same.

4. IMMIGRATION AND DISCRIMINATION: SOME ECONOMIC ASPECTS

DAVID COLLARD
University of Bristol

THE AUTHOR

David Collard, M.A. (Cantab.), was born in 1937 and educated at
Tiverton Grammar School, Devon and Queens' College, Cambridge.
Lecturer in Economics at Bristol University, previously lectured at
University College, Cardiff. Apart from journal articles has written
an introduction to *Mathematical Investigations* by J. Tozer (1838),
published by Augustus Kelly (1968), and edits the *History of Economic Thought Newsletter.* He is author of *The New Right: A Critique,*
Fabian Tract 387 (1968) and his *Prices, Markets and Welfare,* to be
published by Faber and Faber, is forthcoming.

ACKNOWLEDGEMENTS

I wish to thank my colleagues P. J. O'Leary and A. A. Brewer, the
graduate seminar at Sussex University and several friends in the
Labour and Fabian movements for their helpful comments. They
are, of course, in no way responsible for remaining errors.

D. C.

I. WHOSE WELFARE?

Whether or not immigration is a good thing depends mainly on the criterion chosen, from the brotherhood of man to the selling price of one's house. Even on narrowly economic grounds there are many possible criteria—principally the rates of economic growth and of *per capita* incomes in the UK, the countries of origin and the world as a whole, together with any distributional effects within and between countries. Now there is no objective rule to say which of these bundles of criteria is the most important. As it happens much recent discussion has concerned itself solely with economic effects on the UK. Although the greater part of what I have to say in this essay concerns the UK, I shall also say a little about the wider issues and the reader is asked to remember that the choice of criterion is (in current jargon) 'value-loaded'.

The most powerful argument I have seen for taking a purely cosmopolitan point of view has been put by Professor Harry Johnson[1] (in the related but rather different context of the 'brain drain'). The argument is that freedom of factor movements across national boundaries tends to produce equal marginal value productivities everywhere and therefore enables a necessary condition for the maximisation of *world income* to be satisfied. If it is in people's own interests to move, then their money gain indicates the money value of the consequent increase in world income. This desirable outcome is hindered by attempts to control factor movements. The policy presumption is therefore in favour of open-door policies. Scientists should go from the UK to America if they can earn bigger salaries, Jamaican labourers should go to the UK if they can earn bigger wages. It seems to me that one really must end up in a position something like Johnson's if one starts from a cosmopolitan free-market economics standpoint. (Mr. J. Enoch Powell, who takes a consistently free market view on everything from the health service to floating exchange rates but at the same time a restrictive view of a free international market in labour, can presumably be described as an insular free marketeer.) Johnson tempers his argument only to the extent of allowing that substantial costs (externalities) may be associated with emigration from developing countries and that some device might be needed (based perhaps on student loans in the brain drain case) to permit the payment of compensation.

---

[1] H. G. Johnson, 'An Internationalist Model' in W. Adams (ed.), *The Brain Drain,* Macmillan, 1968.

All free market arguments are open to a number of well-known objections. The existing distribution of world income is certainly not acceptable to everybody! There are many distortions and imperfections in trade as well as in factor movements. There are social costs and benefits which cannot easily be taken into account by the market. Thus while an open-door immigration policy is certainly consistent with a free market philosophy I would prefer not to argue for it on that ground.

More importantly, there is the straightforward 'nationalistic' argument that people are much more interested in their own per capita incomes than in those of foreigners. Consequently from the policy-making point of view it is as well to accept that governments will give the incomes of their own nationals a much higher weighting than the incomes of foreigners. The emphasis in this paper will therefore be on per capita incomes in the UK.

There follows: a brief outline of the scale and nature of immigration into the UK, a longer discussion of the macro-economic effects of immigration, an examination of the micro-economic foundations of racial discrimination, and a brief evaluation of the thesis that discrimination is associated with socialism. There is also a short concluding section.

II.   ORDERS OF MAGNITUDE

The Registrar-General has recently improved the factual basis on which statistical questions about the pattern of immigrants' lives can be answered.[1] Information about the annual flow of immigrants continues to be provided under the Commonwealth Immigrants Act,[2] though some observers believe these to be under-estimates.

Importance of statistics

The very fact that this type of statistical information has been collected is highly significant. One learns from workers in the field that up to the early 1960s (or possibly only up to the Notting Hill riots of 1958) not only were detailed statistics not available but their very collection was felt to be a bad thing as it would only exacerbate racial tensions. Now that they are available I believe that wider publication can only help. They show that the absolute size of the problem is rather less impressive than its crisis headlines sug-

---

[1]   *Sample Census 1966. Commonwealth Immigrant Tables,* HMSO, 1969.

[2]   *Commonwealth Immigrants Act 1962. Control of Immigration, Statistics,* HMSO (normally available in April).

gest, that it is not likely to grow much as a result of further immigration (though the immigrant population will grow relatively quickly at first due to its unusual age distribution and pre-assimilation higher fertility rates), and that the job distribution by industry group is not strikingly different from that warranted by the existing structure of jobs and the need for newcomers to go where there are job opportunities. The worrying parts of the problem are the difficulties that coloured immigrants face in moving up the socio-economic scale and their experiences in housing and similar markets.

I shall be concerned only with what the Registrar General calls 'New Commonwealth' immigrants. For present purposes I shall use the categories 'New Commonwealth' and 'coloured' as synonymous. Almost 80 per cent of coloured immigrants come from three broad areas: India-Pakistan (37 per cent), British Caribbean (32 per cent) and Africa (10 per cent). The *stock* consisted in 1966 of about 480,000 males and 370,000 females, that is about 850,000 in total or 1.8 per cent of the population of England and Wales. The aggregate percentage, therefore, is still quite small.

Figure I shows that the *flow* of all immigrants abated after the 1962 Commonwealth Immigrants Act. A detailed breakdown of the 1968

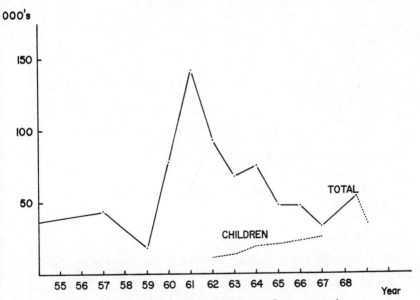

Fig I. Commonwealth immigrants: net inward movement

Sources: *Commonwealth Immigrants Act 1962 (Statistics)*, op. cit.
R. B. Davison, *Black British Immigrants to England*, Oxford, 1966.

69

figure is not available at the time of writing but the indications are
that the net inward movement of males was very small (for Jamaican men it was negative in 1967), most of the immigrants being
children (persons under 16) or women coming to join their families.
Given present legislation it is reasonable to expect that when this
process has worked itself through the net inward movement will
become extremely small.

The unusual family structure during the early period of immigration means that over 80 per cent of immigrants can be classified as
economically active. Only 2 per cent are over 65 compared with
12 per cent for the population as a whole (Table 1). There is every
reason to expect that the distribution will become more normal as
children continue to join their families and as those immigrants at
work approach retiring age.

**TABLE 1 Age Distribution of 'New Common-
wealth' Immigrants and UK Population, 1966**

		per cent	
Age	*N/C Immigrants*		*UK Population*
0-14	17		23
15-64*	81		65
65+	2		12
Total	100		100

Sources: *Commonwealth Immigrants Act 1962.
Control of Immigration Statistics,*
HMSO, and *Annual Abstract of Sta-
tistics 1967,* HMSO.

* This figure is often referred to as the 'activity rate'.

Geographic and job distribution

Where do they live? The most striking thing about the regional distribution of coloured immigrants is not their concentration in the
West Midlands but the overwhelming importance of Greater London
where 43 per cent of them lived in 1966 (Table 2). Contrary to
popular opinion the rate of owner-occupation of houses is higher
among immigrants (especially Indians) than among the population
at large, but the popular view of overcrowding is confirmed. Immigrants take jobs which place them typically lower down the economic

TABLE 2 Regional Distribution of 'New Commonwealth' Immigrants and UK Population, 1966

per cent

Area	N/C Immigrants	All UK Citizens
London	43	15
Other South East	15	17
West Midlands	13	9
Total for 3 areas	71	41

Sources: As for Table 1.

scale than the population as a whole. The difference is not spectacular at the extreme ends of the scale but, as studies of discrimination have indicated, is very important at the divide between semi-skilled manual labour and non-manual jobs (that is, between classes 5 and 4: Table 3). Thus 26 per cent of coloured immigrants are in the service and semi-skilled manual labour category but only 14 per cent of the population as a whole.

Popular impressions of the job distribution of coloured immigrants are based on those the public happens to come into contact with, such as bus conductors and nurses. The distribution is, however, much more 'normal' than these impressions would lead one to ex-

TABLE 3 Greater London Socio-Economic Groups: Males, 1966

per cent

Socio-Economic Group	N/C Immigrants	Whole Population
1. Professional	6	5
2. Employers, Managers	4	12
3. Foremen, Skilled Manual, etc.	33	34
4. Non-Manual	17	23
5. Service etc., Semi-Skilled Manual	26	14
6. Unskilled Manual	13	8

Source: *New Society,* 26 June, 1969, based on *Commonwealth Immigrants Act 1962* etc., *op. cit.* (Figures do not add to 100%.)

pect (Table 4). There are a great many labourers and engineering
workers but very few clerks (again the literature on discrimination
is relevant). Notice that only 2 per cent are classified as bus conductors! The pattern for female immigrants is rather different, over
60 per cent of them falling into the three categories, professional,
service and clerical. The popular view of their importance to the
hospital service is confirmed by the figure of 17 per cent as nurses.
The important thing is not the job distribution of immigrants but
how it compares with the distribution for the whole population. I
have calculated 'weights' for each industry group showing the number
of immigrants as a percentage of the whole work force and separated
out those with a high and those with a low weight (Table 5 (a) and (b)).
Notice the very small number of immigrants in mining and agricul-
ture and the relatively high percentage (up to 5.3) in various types
of manufacturing. This spread is consistent with the hypothesis
that immigrants go where there are labour 'shortages'.

Employment data can be used to support the hypothesis that immigrant labour has been unusually responsive to the changing struc-

TABLE 4 (A) Principal Employment of Male Immigrants, 1966

Industry Group		% of Total Male Immigrants
XVIII	Labourers (nec)	16
VII	Engineering and Allied Trade workers (nec)	15
XXV	Professional, etc.	10
XIX	Transport, etc.	9
	[Bus Conductors	2]
XXIII	Service, etc.	8
XXI	Clerical	6

(B) Principal Employment of Female Immigrants, 1966

Industry Group		% of Total Female Immigrants
XXV	Professional, etc.	23
	[Nurses	17]
XXIII	Service, etc.	20
XXI	Clerical	18

Source: Commonwealth Immigrants Act 1962 etc., op. cit.

TABLE 5

(A) Industry Groups with a High 'Weighting' of Immigrant Workers

Industry Group	Weight *per cent*
16 Other Manufacturing	5.3
10 Textiles	5.3
11 Leather	4.6
12 Clothing	4.6
5 Metals	4.0
9 Metal (nes)	4.0

(B) Industry Groups with a Low 'Weighting' of Immigrant Workers

Industry Group	Weight *per cent*
18 Gas, Electricity	1.1
1 Agriculture	0.4
2 Mining	0.2

Sources: *Commenwealth Immigrants Act 1962 etc., op. cit.,* and *Statistics on Incomes, Prices, Employment and Production,* No. 20, March 1967.

ture of industry. In the period 1960-66 some occupations grew, others declined. Generally there was no definite relationship between the size of an occupation group (by employment) and the extent of its expansion or contraction. This can be seen by casual inspection of a scatter diagram of 1966 labour force against the change in the labour force from 1960 to 1966 in each main occupational group.[1] However, the male immigrant labour force does seem to have responded positively to expansion or contraction (if the figure for 'transport' is neglected). The regression equation is

$$y = 11.2 + 0.08 x$$

where y and x are immigrant labour and the change in male labour force (000s). The correlation coefficient is low (+0.58) but significant, reflecting the fact that a number of causes must operate on the distribution of immigrant labour apart from x. The coefficient for x suggests that 8 per cent of any occupational expansion or contraction has been met by immigrant labour, a much higher percentage than the relative size of the immigrant force would indicate.

---

[1] The sources are *Commonwealth Immigrant Tables: 1966 Sample Census; Statistics on Incomes, Prices, Employment and Production.*

III. MACRO-ECONOMIC EFFECTS

(a) The growth rate

A steady stream of immigrants raises the rate of growth of a country's working population. If the home population is growing at 1 per cent per annum and the annual stream of immigrants is equal to 0.1 per cent of the home population, the rate of total population growth is 1.1 per cent. If immigrants are more fertile than the indigenous population the rate would be raised still further (but we have already suggested that this may not be an important factor in the longer term). The effect of an increased population growth upon the rate of *economic* growth will depend on what is happening to the rate of growth of productivity. If it remains unchanged the rate of economic growth will be lifted by 0.1 per cent.[1]

A once and for all burst of immigration (as opposed to a steady flow) will cause output to be permanently higher, for it is hardly credible that the extra labour would have a negative productivity. But it cannot, directly, have any effect on the rate of growth of output.

(b) Inflation

Although immigration increases the total of real resources available it is possible that it also stimulates an even larger demand for resources so that the net effect is inflationary, especially in the short term. Opposing conclusions have been reached. Thus Professor Charles Kindleberger states[2] that 'high rates of savings and of remittance abroad of the average immigrant make him contribute more to supply than to demand and thus hold down inflation', while Dr. E.J. Mishan and L. Needleman[3] are more pessimistic. Kindleberger argues that labour supplies were an overwhelmingly important ingredient of Europe's post-war economic growth. The great migratory movements within Europe eased supply bottlenecks and, by keeping wages low, raised profit expectations and therefore investment. A deflationary impact is entirely consistent with (and probably necessary to) his thesis.

---

[1] The 'natural' rate of growth equals the rate of growth of working population *plus* the rate of growth of productivity. For example, 4.1% = 1.1% + 3.0%. If the rate of growth of productivity fell by 0.1% (simultaneously) the growth rate would revert to 4%.

[2] C.P. Kindleberger, *Europe's Postwar Growth. The Role of Labour Supply,* Harvard University Press, 1967.

[3] E.J. Mishan and L. Needleman, 'Immigration, Excess Demand and the Balance of Payments', *Economica,* May, 1966.

Mishan and Needleman, on the other hand, argue that there will be substantial excess demand particularly in the early years. This is not the place for a full analysis of their carefully worked out macro-economic model. I would argue, however, that their pessimistic conclusion depends crucially upon the *investment expenditure* generated in consequence of a new immigrant family. It is reasonable to suppose that there will be some *investment demand* for new machinery or plant and also for social overhead capital. Astonishingly, the authors assume that

(1) each immigrant family will be provided with a stock of social and industrial capital equal to the average ($\lambda = 1$);

(2) this capital will be provided over a period of two years ($t = 2$).

Each of these assumptions is, of course, open to serious challenge. There is plenty of evidence that immigrants have to make do, over quite a long period, with inferior social capital. Kindleberger certainly takes this view.

> 'Because the foreign workers will accept low levels of accommodation—without their families and the concomitant need for schools, hospitals and housing—investment in social overhead capital can be kept relatively low.'

It can also, unfortunately, be kept relatively low even after their families arrive. Admittedly some social costs will be high (for example, the rare use of small specialist classes equipped with tape-recorders, for the learning of English) but there is evidence that old schools have been re-opened, that those scheduled for closure have been kept open, and so on.[1] Though the operating costs of these schools may be high the capital costs will be negligible.

Clearly it would be sensible to assume a lower value of λ and also a longer period for building up the new level of capital. On Mishan and Needleman's calculations investment demand generated by a single family is of the order of £3,000 per annum. Taking (for example) instead a value of $\lambda = 0.75$ and $t = 5$, investment demand would be only £900. The result is therefore very sensitive to changes in these important assumptions.

Two things can be said. First, it is not certain that there will be any inflationary impact. Second, over the years governments have to put up with shifts in excess demand resulting from all sorts of causes. One of the major jobs of short-run macro-economic policy

---

1 T. F. Davies, 'Educational Problems in Bradford' in G. E. W. Wolstenholme (ed.), *Immigration, Medical and Social Aspects,* Ciba Foundation, 1966.

is to adjust to these changes by appropriate monetary and fiscal measures. If excess demand is generated there has (in real terms) to be a small net flow of resources towards the immigrant families; whether the current consumption of the rest of the population is (slightly) reduced by rising prices, higher taxes or monetary restraint is outside the scope of this essay.

(c) Per capita income

To establish the likely effect of sustained immigration on income per head we need a model of some kind. One of the simplest makes use of the so-called 'neo-classical' production function. Output is said to be a function of factor supplies (labour and capital) and technical progress and may or may not be subject to economies of scale. Immigration implies an increase in *one* factor, labour. This will certainly increase output but, owing to diminishing marginal returns to each factor, may or may not increase output per head (the *average* product of labour). Diminishing marginal returns can, however, be offset by economies of scale (indicated by writing $V > 1$ in the model).

A neo-classical model of this type was used by Mishan and Needleman.[1,2] They conclude,

> 'the range of calculations... will suggest to all the need for more restraint than has been shown in the last few years by financial journals. Certainly no support is lent by this part of our analysis to the frequent allegation that immigration into the UK confers economic benefits on the existing inhabitants—if anything the analysis tends to point the other way'.

They select a value for V between 1.0 and 1.2, with which it is difficult to quarrel.[3] A much higher V would, of course, ensure rising output per head.

In this type of model capital and labour are substitutes for one another so that as the labour-capital ratio rises more labour-using

---

[1] E. J. Mishan and L. Needleman, 'Immigration: Some Long Term Economic Consequences', *Economia Internazionale,* Pt. A: Vol. XXI, No. 2, May 1968; Part B: Vol. XXI, No. 3, August 1968.

[2] E. J. Mishan and L. Needleman, 'Immigration: Long-Run Economic Effects', *Lloyds Bank Review,* January 1968. This is a popularised version of the articles in the previous footnote.

[3] Cf. E. F. Denison, *Why Growth Rates Differ: Post-War Experience in Nine Western Countries,* Brookings Institution, Washington, D.C., 1967.

techniques of production are employed. Now suppose a rather different model (which I shall call the Kindleberger-Lewis-Marx, or KLM model) in which entrepreneurs wish to invest (expand the stock of capital) but

(1) capital and labour can be used only in fixed proportion to one another;

(2) indigeneous labour cannot be increased sufficiently quickly to 'man-up' the new capital which entrepreneurs wish to create.

In this situation immigration breaks the labour supply constraint and permits the capital stock to increase. An increase in labour is, in a sense, the cause of the increase in capital. A model of this kind is implied in Kindleberger,[1] where economic growth sustains itself by drawing in excess supplies of labour from the countryside or from other countries. If these supplies dry up then a brake is put on the process of 'super-growth'. Notice a curious inconsistency between the short- and long-run models of Mishan and Needleman; in the short term there is a constant proportion between labour and capital stock (the creation of which is inflationary) while in the longer term the labour-capital ratio simply increases.

Another case in which increased labour supplies might cause an increase in the rate of growth of capital would be if they caused the rate of profit on capital to rise (or, effectively, redistributed income away from workers), thus stimulating entrepreneurs to invest. Kindleberger clearly puts great emphasis on this effect but, as we shall see in the next section, there is no reason for believing that it is quantitatively important in the UK.

Finally, immigration will mean that labour is relatively plentiful. This will cause existing plant to be worked more intensively and perhaps discourage the search for new labour-saving techniques. Investment will continue (there will be 'capital-widening') but it will be relatively labour using (there will not be much 'capital-deepening'). Some writers have alleged that in public transport immigrant labour has weakened the incentive to explore new methods—single fares, one-man buses, etc. Our analysis on pages 72-3 gives some support to this view as, it will be remembered, 'transport' was left out of the regression analysis on the ground that it did not fit. But there is some misunderstanding of this point. If, for some reason, labour becomes plentiful it is efficient to use the more labour intensive of existing techniques. This may cause per capita income to fall but has been dealt with already in the production function analysis; to deal with it again in another guise would be double-counting. It can

---

[1] *Op. cit.*, Ch. I.

only be a further disadvantage if it slows up the rate of growth of technical progress.

Evidence of a brake on technical progress would need gathering right across the board and the information we have is scanty indeed. Kindleberger in his European study found the evidence to be rather mixed. Thus in the UK slow rates of labour growth have been accompanied by slow increases in productivity; in Germany fast rates of labour growth by fast increases in productivity; in France the rate of growth of productivity seems to have been pretty well independent of labour supplies; while in Switzerland there is some evidence that immigration did slow down the rate of capital-deepening.

To summarise:

(1) Conclusions on *per capita* income depend crucially on the type of model chosen.

(2) The effects are not likely to be large.

(3) Before generalising one needs to know more about
     (a) the causal relationship between labour supplies and investment;
     (b) the causal relationship between labour supplies and technical progress.

(d) Income redistribution

It is not sensible to talk about income redistribution in terms of the two classes capital and labour. Let us distinguish, crudely, four main 'classes'. The degree to which factors of production are in competition with one another is given by the 'elasticity of substitution', the greater the elasticity of substitution (e) the more will the earnings of other factors be affected by increased labour supplies. In Figure II I distinguish between high, medium and low e's.

	(i)	(ii)	(iii)
(i) Immigrant Labour			
(ii) Unskilled Labour	High		
(iii) Skilled Labour	Med.	Med.	
(iv) Capital	Low	Low	Med.

FIG. II.   Conjectured elasticities of substitution (e's) between various groups

78

If this scheme is even roughly correct there are some factors of production (owners of skilled labour and of capital goods) which, as far as immigrant labour is concerned, will be non-competing groups. If the price mechanism works properly, indigeneous unskilled labour will lose relatively to non-competing groups of skilled indigeneous labour and to indigeneous owners of capital. The redistributive effect of immigration will be regressive though, at full employment with strong trade unions and highly imperfect factor markets, it may not be quantitatively significant.

Unskilled and semi-skilled workers in areas of high immigrant con-centration are likely to be adversely affected. As is suggested in pages 84-5, this could account for more apparent colour prejudice among working-class than among middle-class groups and is often too lightly dismissed by liberals. But the problem is really part of the wider problem of low pay and redundancy; the real or imagined costs to unskilled workers of a freer immigration policy can be reduced by higher social security benefits, minimum wage legislation and generous redundancy pay. One hesitates to 'recommend' a policy that may make people as a whole better off but may also make the poorer members of the community worse off. It is up to the rest of us to make sure that that does not happen.

(e) Balance of payments

At first sight the behaviour of exports might be assumed entirely exogenous except in one small respect—that remittances and immi-grant-induced imports will themselves induce UK exports. Let us make this assumption for the moment. It then follows that both in the long and the short term the effect of immigration on the balance of payments will be unfavourable; for as population and income rise, so do imports. In real terms this implies a redistribution of goods from this country to the rest of the world and the mechanism by which this is achieved is outside our present scope.

Now relax the assumption that exports are exogenous.[1] We have already suggested that immigrant labour has a role to play in break-ing labour 'bottlenecks' (note that under neo-classical conditions there can be no bottlenecks). I am not now suggesting that supply difficulties are the only, or even the most important, determinant of exports but simply that some kind of labour supply variable should be put into the equation determining imports. One hypothesis worthy of study is that the higher the degree of mobility or adaptability in a country's labour force the more effectively will it be able to re-spond to changes in comparative advantage.

---

[1] This assumption accounts for some of the more pessimistic long-run results obtained by Mishan and Needleman.

To summarise:

(1) Demonstrations of an adverse effect on the balance of payments depend on the exogeneous behaviour of exports.

(2) We need to know more about the relationship between labour supplies and exports.

(f) Country of origin

Putting the production function model into reverse we might expect per capita income to rise in the country of origin and the distribution of income to improve—that is, to move in favour of labour as against capital. The KLM model is not 'reversible'. The country of origin has an 'excess' of labour so both countries gain. Thus whether the KLM or production function model is used there will be an 'improvement' in the country of origin. Immigration is therefore a good thing and serves as a partial substitute for foreign aid.

While I am in favour of a more liberal immigration policy than we at present operate in the UK I really doubt that the country of origin (as opposed to the immigrants themselves) gains very much. In Table 6 I have chosen some statistics for two important countries of origin, India and Jamaica. These countries have low levels of real income compared with the UK and high rates of population growth. Assuming recent growth rates of population continue we can expect annual increases in population of the order of 12 million in India and 50, 000 in Jamaica. Set against the British figure for annual immigration (approximately 50, 000) it is clear that marginal increases in immigration into Britain would have trivial effects on

TABLE 6 Population Growth and Real Income in Jamaica, India and England and Wales, 1967

Country	Population (1)	Rate of Growth of Population (2)	'Annual Increase' (1) × (2)	Per Capita Income
	million	%	000s	$
Jamaica	1.84	2.7	50	427
India	499	2.4	12, 000	79
England & Wales	48	0.7	335	1, 517

Source: *United Nations Statistical Year Book 1967,* New York, 1968 (principally Table 17).

the pressure of population in India and only small effects on the pressure of population in Jamaica.

More contentious is the question of whether the countries of origin are harmed by the loss of skilled people. At the top level this is labelled 'brain drain' and is principally a flow to the USA. The main British experience of this type of immigrant relates to Indian or Pakistani doctors. Lower down the socio-economic scale those who are well enough off to get the fares together and enterprising enough to get away are among the more valuable members of society. It could be then that a brain drain (or more accurately a skill drain) has harmful effects out of all proportion to the numbers involved.

There are two reasons for believing that such harm can be exaggerated. The first is a little speculative and has already been briefly discussed. It derives from cosmopolitanism. At the crudest level it simply puts aside nationalistic considerations, taking instead a world view. At a more sophisticated level it suggests that knowledge and skill (once developed) are common property and it is best for people to go where the efficiency of their contribution will be largest. This public property of knowledge is very much less true of business than of university research and I suspect that much recent optimistic cosmopolitanism has reflected a debate confined very largely within university circles. The other reason is rather more convincing and has been put by Professor H. Myint.[1] It is that, for reasons of prestige, the manpower balance as between supply and demand has been upset. More engineers, doctors, etc., have been produced than the home economy can absorb at anything like current salary levels. (This is associated with the phenomenon of the 'mob'— those with university degrees but no special skills.) The implication is that these people, because of their over-production, have very low marginal productivities at home so that by losing them the country does not lose very much. If they work abroad and send remittances and if they add to the world stock of knowledge there might even be a gain.

I have said enough, I think, to show that the problem is rather complex. My own feeling is that in general those developing countries which export skilled labour are probably losing out in terms of real income per head. But it would be useless to block the outflow without at the same time effecting such a redistribution of incomes between countries as to permit some of the skilled people to be employed at home. It is politically naive to advocate more aid as a replacement for immigration into the UK, for a political party which takes a tough line on immigration is also likely to take a tough line on foreign aid.

---

[1] H. Myint, 'A Less Alarmist View', in W. Adams (ed.), *The Brain Drain*, *op. cit.*

⟵ IV. ECONOMICS OF DISCRIMINATION

We have already seen that from a world point of view barriers to
labour movements prevent an efficient allocation of resources. We
have also seen that this consideration will not impress a government interested in the per capita incomes of its own nationals. How
much immigration control will individual voters prefer? I suggest
that this depends on two things, the individual's 'taste' for control
and his beliefs about the economic effects of immigration. I also
suggest the same framework for discussing the amount of discrimination within the UK.

Degree of discrimination

Evidence that discrimination exists is overwhelming. The well-
known PEP report[1] sought evidence from those who were likely to
be discriminated against and those who were in positions to be able
to discriminate, following this up by a number of carefully controlled
situation tests. Surprisingly, immigrants tended to *under-state* the
amount of discrimination (partly because many of them avoid po-
tentially discriminatory situations). Those who discriminated had in
mind a few simple racial stereotypes based on hearsay and their
own worst kinds of experience: the immigrant is dirty, he has a chip-
on-his-shoulder, he is badly educated, he is immoral, he is obsessed
by sex, etc. As between immigrant groups the Indians are rather
better regarded than, say, the West Indians, but within each group
there is little attempt to treat applicants for jobs, houses and so on
as individuals rather than just 'coloureds'. Sexual fears and a horror
of physical contact show themselves in a reluctance to use coloured
workers (until recently) in food handling or underwear sales and
attempts to set up separate toilet and eating facilities in some fac-
tories. As a general rule discrimination is greater the more senior
the position and the closer the personal contact. In housing there is
'massive discrimination' based solely on colour. Many of these
types of discrimination are, of course, now illegal in principle—it
would be interesting to know how much difference this had made in
practice.

Causes of job discrimination

In the job market immigrants get the worst positions, find promotion
difficult and suffer high rates of unemployment (though often less

---

[1] W. W. Daniel, *Racial Discrimination in England,* Pelican, 1968
(based on the PEP report of 1967).

than in their country of origin). Now *apparent discrimination* can be due to three causes, which I shall discuss in turn: (i) low labour productivity, (ii) low price elasticities of labour supply, and (iii) pure discrimination. Readers who are familiar with Becker's analysis[1] will notice that his 'discrimination coefficient' is intended to cover the last of these.

(i)   *Low labour productivity*

It would be unrealistic to deny that in the early years of immigration some of the new workers will be less productive than their 'white' workmates. Their English may be poor, they may be unused to the discipline of factory life. Thus it is alleged[2] that, whereas Anglo-Indians and Poles are good workers, West Indians are slow, inefficient and prone to absence in bad weather. The trouble with this explanation is that it cannot be pushed very far. We have already seen that the more educated the immigrant the more likely he is to encounter discrimination. Further the use of 'stereotypes' ensures that employers often have quite mistaken ideas about the immigrant's ability. Those who try immigrants often revise their opinions upwards. Unfortunately employment prospects depend not on the productivity of the immigrant but on what the employer believes his productivity to be. An employer's own racial prejudices often take the form of *believing* that immigrants are inefficient, that white workers would not tolerate them and that customers would not stand for it. In so far as these beliefs are false one can be optimistic about the longer-run prospect. The really worrying thing is that some discrimination persists into the next generation; discrimination against English-educated and 'culture-assimilated' coloured school-leavers really has to be explained in terms of residual pure discrimination.

(ii)   *Low price-elasticities of labour supply*

Immigrants (like women) may be discriminated against in the job market because they will not withdraw when less attractive positions are offered. Again, this is something I would not expect to persist for long since it is a feature of the early years when the male immigrant is saving so as to bring his family over and perhaps buy a house. Thus Jamaicans commonly remit home 10-15 per cent of

---

1   G. S. Becker, *The Economics of Discrimination*, Chicago, 1967.

2   S. Patterson, *Immigrants in Industry*, published for the Institute of Race Relations by Oxford University Press, 1968. This study of integration in Croydon lays stress on slow continuous improvement.

their pay.[1] Indians, says Desai,[2] send remittances home in order to maintain status in the eyes of an extended family group (and perhaps ease the path to marriage). House-buying is a major motive for saving: according to the 1966 census 58 per cent of Indian households are owner-occupied. Immigrants are extremely keen to get overtime work.

This high-saving pattern is a feature of the very unusual age structure of immigrants (Table 1) and of the pioneering role of the male. As families come over to join the head of household we would expect the early phase of high accumulation to give way to more normal consumption patterns. Also trade unions are now in the forefront of attacks on racial discrimination. Understandably this was not so in the earlier years as local labour has a great deal more to lose than local management.[3] More discrimination may not involve more prejudice but simply different economic interests. Informal agreements and even quotas have been used as protective devices. But the present tendency is to accept coloured workers into the usual union structure without discrimination. Finally, government legislation has reduced immigration to a mere trickle, thus improving the market position of existing immigrants.

(iii) *Pure discrimination*

I have given my reasons for expecting discrimination from causes (i) and (ii) to disappear within a reasonable period of time. This brings us to the much more serious hard-core of the problem, what I have called pure discrimination. Attitudes elicited during the PEP Survey suggest that this hard-core will remain for quite a long time. A discussion of the factors influencing discrimination might be of some service in pointing to 'solutions'. The amount of discrimination which people practise is determined by two separate factors,

    (1) their 'taste' for discrimination;

    (2) the 'price' of discrimination.

If this is granted, the ordinary analysis of consumer demand can be applied (the reader who finds such devices helpful is referred to the

---

[1] R. B. Davison, *Black British Immigrants to England,* Oxford, 1966. This study provides much detailed information about Jamaicans, using an ingenious method to obtain a random sample.

[2] R. Desai, *Indian Immigrants in Britain,* published for the Institute of Race Relations by Oxford University Press, 1963—an intimate account of Indian communities in this country.

[3] Discussed above, page 79, and in (iii) below.

indifference curves in the footnote).[1] A report[2] produced in the summer of 1969 suggested that most people dislike (or are against) discrimination. But the analysis of consumer behaviour suggests that people with anti-discriminatory tastes might, in practice, vote for or carry out discrimination so long as the price of discrimination was 'negative' to them (that is, they gained from it). This seems to be an extremely common category. 'I'm not prejudiced but...'. It covers the paradox of those who practice discrimination but preach non-discrimination—householders who try to prevent 'coloureds' moving into the area because this might bring down house prices, trade unionists who profess brotherhood but try to operate quotas, etc. The position is a routine consequence of utility-maximising behaviour.

In general, actual discrimination can be reduced in the following ways (apart from prohibition):

(1) People must be educated to alter their 'tastes'. Great strides can be made simply by dispelling popular errors (that immigrants smell, urinate in the streets, live on the earnings of prostitutes and so on). Much of this will come through familiarity.

---

1 Let the 'amount' of discrimination be measured on the horizontal axis and 'goods' on the vertical axis.

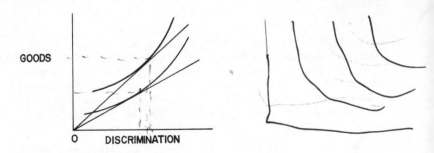

GOODS

O   DISCRIMINATION

FIG. III.   Indifference curves of the cost of discrimination

As discrimination is disliked, the indifference curves rise from left to right. The lines from the origin represent the 'negative price' of discrimination. In the 'normal' case the higher the negative price the more discrimination is practised.

2 *Colour and Citizenship: A Report on British Race Relations,* Institute of Race Relations, 1969. This report appeared after the first draft of the present paper was written. I am much in agreement with the conclusions reached by Professor Maurice Peston in section 31.

(2) Assessments of economic loss due to immigrants, in any case highly uncertain, should certainly not err on the pessimistic side. The more people believe that they will lose the more likely they are *(whatever their basic prejudices)* to support discriminatory policies.

(3) Where particular groups actually gain by discrimination there may *possibly* be a case for compensating them when public policy moves in favour of non-discrimination. Otherwise any economic 'burden' is unfairly shared.

Discrimination has been discussed as though it depended entirely on individual decisions and for many types of discrimination this is certainly so. But discrimination *par excellence* is operated through immigration control and is beyond the decisions of individuals. (In technical terms it is a 'public good' whose amount is, in the simplest of models, determined by the preferences of the median voter). Action under the three headings above should cause public opinion to move in favour of a rather more lenient immigration policy.

The Hutt thesis

Professor W. H. Hutt has put forward the curious thesis that racial discrimination is associated with socialism.[1]

'The survival of apartheid is, indeed, the survival of a kind of socialism—often altruistically motivated—whilst the dissolution of colour injustice has been continuously assisted by competitive capitalism'.

Entrepreneurs, he argues, will (under competitive conditions) be anxious to keep costs of production at a minimum. To discriminate, for instance by restricting the movement of labour, will be against their self-interest; such pressures are absent under socialism and consequently it will be easier to maintain discrimination. Hutt illustrates his thesis from historical experience ranging from medieval Jewry to contemporary *apartheid*.

The central defect of Hutt's proposition is that it ignores what I have called the hard core of the problem, pure discrimination. If consumers have tastes which favour discrimination (if they are prejudiced, that is) entrepreneurs will, in a free enterprise system, find it in their interests to pander to these tastes. Essentially Hutt sees discrimination as a feature of economic disequilibrium. But if consumers are prejudiced discrimination must be a feature of *equilibrium*. On this *a priori* ground, as well as on grounds of casual empiricism, Hutt's thesis must be rejected.

---

[1] W. H. Hutt, *The Economics of the Colour Bar*, Institute of Economic Affairs, 1964.

The grain of truth in his analysis is that the extent of discrimination will (as we have seen) tend to vary inversely with its economic cost. People will discriminate less if they meet economic disadvantage on the way. As the major kinds of discrimination (immigration control, *apartheid*) are matters of public policy there is no reason why the response to these economic disadvantages should be stronger under capitalism than under socialism.

V. SUMMARY AND CONCLUSIONS

Generally I feel that current discussions of the economics of immigration are too narrow and too gloomy. The small and highly conjectural gains and losses seem trivial when set beside the problem of race relations in a multi-racial community. Perhaps the economist can contribute a little by trying to put the issues in perspective. I offer the following conclusions.

1. Alarmist views about the racial position in this country ignore the fact that really new immigration has been reduced almost to a trickle. At present we are seeing a gradual normalisation of the immigrant age and family structure.

2. A flow of immigrant labour will increase total output and a steady flow, proportionate to existing population, will probably increase the rate of growth of output.

3. In the present state of the art economists can say very little about the longer-run effects of immigration on income per head.

4. Some estimates of the inflationary effects of immigration have erred very much on the side of pessimism.

5. Large-scale immigration would have the effect of redistributing income away from those workers with whom the immigrants were in direct competition. To the limited extent that this occurs already the solution is an attack on the whole problem of low wages, not an attack on the role of the immigrant.

6. As the numbers are small in relation to population increases in the countries of origin, increased immigration can have no significant effect in relieving population pressures. On the contrary, loss of skilled people may have an adverse effect (though this is controversial).

7. The amount of discrimination practised by individuals (or supported through the ballot box) depends on the imagined 'price' of discriminating as well as on prejudice itself. Education, familiarity and so on can do much to reduce the amount of prejudice; but just as important is the dispelling of gloomy economic predictions of its effects.

5. DOES IMMIGRATION CONFER ECONOMIC BENEFITS ON THE HOST COUNTRY?*

E. J. MISHAN
University of London

* I am indebted to Mr Arthur Seldon for a number of suggestions
that have substantially improved the exposition.

THE AUTHOR

Dr E. J. Mishan, B.A.(Manchester), Ph.D.(Chicago), M.Sc.(Economics), was born November 1917 and educated at Manchester Grammar School and Manchester University. He is Reader in Economics at the London School of Economics. At present he is at the American University, Washington, D.C.

Apart from numerous journal articles he is author of *The Costs of Economic Growth*, Staples Press, 1967; *Growth: The Price We Pay*, Staples Press, 1969; *Welfare Economics*, Random Press, 1965; and *21 Popular Economic Fallacies*, Allen Lane, the Penguin Press, 1969.

INTRODUCTORY REMARKS

The economic aspects of immigration, like those of any other social phenomenon, can be treated either as a positive ('behaviourist') or a 'normative' ('prescriptive' or 'policy-oriented') study. A positive study of immigration may be either historic and descriptive, or else analytic. If the latter, it will concern itself mainly with the impact of migration on resource and product prices. A normative study, on the other hand, will comprehend economic analysis and with its aid seek to appraise the results in terms of 'better' or 'worse', as does the present paper.[1] This it may do within a world context, or else within a regional or national context.

Free trade model

Western economists, whose training begins more often than not with 'ideal' or highly simplified models having such features as universally competitive markets, unrestrained mobility of resources *within* countries (though not between countries), unhindered and costless free trade, tend to favour the promotion of such features in the real world. Nor is this predilection entirely unconscious or irrational: normative studies do appear to endow these 'ideal' features with characteristics that are believed to maximise social welfare.

By simple extension of such features, unimpeded migration of all resources might be justified as tending to realise, under familiar conditions, an increase in world economic efficiency—defined as a situation in which the gains (valued at the resultant world prices) exceed the losses; a definition implying that a costless distribution of the gains *could* in practice make everyone in the world better off.

---

[1] I use normative here only in the sense of selecting several criteria by which economic advantage or disadvantage are commonly judged. A near consensus of informed opinion would regard any increase in the rate of inflation or in the trade deficit as, of itself, undesirable. Turning to long-term consequences, few would dissent from the view that any retardation of the growth of per capita income among the indigenous population, or any regressive tendency in distribution of the national product, is of itself undesirable. It is, of course, possible to be unimpressed by such criteria without being critical of the results of the analysis. The reverse is also possible: the criteria may be readily acceptable while remaining sceptical of the validity of the analysis.

The logic that tends to this conclusion is simple to illustrate. If, for example, £1 million of capital which could earn 6 per cent per annum in Western Europe is transferred to somewhere in South East Asia where, after allowance for additional risk, it earns 15 per cent per annum, its transfer from Western Europe to that area increases world income by 9 per cent of £1 million or £90,000 per annum. Again, if an unskilled worker in Madras earning the equivalent of £3 per week moves to Britain and earns £20 per week, world 'real' income rises by £17 per week. In sum, so long as real differentials in the earnings of resources exist between different areas of the world there would appear to be scope for increasing world GNP.

What is true for the whole, however, is not necessarily true for each of the parties comprising it. Just as the doctrine that free trade is the best policy was qualified for a single country soon after the turn of the century[1]—a qualification that was the harbinger of the growing interest, in the 'forties and 'fifties, of 'optimal' tariffs—so also must the proposition that unhindered migration raises 'real' income be qualified in the case of single countries.

In one respect, however, there is a difference between the free mobility of goods and that of resources. A set of tariffs which raises the welfare of a country as compared with free trade obviously requires the continued existence of some international trade. Indeed such tariffs are consistent with a country increasing its foreign trade over the years. In contrast, the degree of immigration that would maximise the welfare of the host country as compared with unlimited free entry could be zero:[2] it is *possible*, that is, that no immigration at all is the optimum immigration policy, or, for that matter, a policy of net emigration. It is *possible* then that any inflow of labour entails a loss of welfare for the *host country*, notwithstanding that *world* welfare is raised by the migration.

Economic benefits or losses of immigration

Let us now turn to consider the net economic benefits or losses arising from immigration in the host country, with particular re-

---

[1] For instance by Bickerdike in *The Economic Journal*, 1906. His reluctance to break with the traditional view of free trade can be gauged to some extent by the title of his article 'The Theory of Incipient Taxes', and the impression he conveyed that the analysis was more of a curiosum than a contribution to economic policy.

[2] Abstracting from theoretical schemes for exploiting immigrant labour by imposing on it differential taxes. In this connection see, for instance, Y. K. Ramaswami, 'International Factor Movement and the National Advantage', *Economica*, August 1968.

ference to Britain. There will be no need to employ sophisticated welfare techniques[1] if we can provide a tentative answer based on widely accepted indices of economic benefit. We can do this for two aspects of the problem:

I. The effects of immigration alone on aggregate demand and on the balance of payments in a relatively inflationary economy over a short period of, say, 10 to 20 years;

II. The effects of immigration alone on per capita real income of the indigenous population and on the distribution of the national product.

In addition, two other aspects may be considered, albeit briefly and informally:

III. The advantages and disadvantages of meeting particular labour shortages by immigrant labour;

IV. The external effects of immigration, broadly conceived.

Before discussing the first two aspects, I and II, a few words on the relevance of the approach adopted here.

(1) We need hardly pause to reject, in such an appraisal, the pertinence of such magnitudes as the contribution to GNP of the immigrant group, or any other group for that matter, and related magnitudes such as total contribution to the Exchequer, or total demand for goods, total contribution to saving, and so on. We could import working population until at the margin the value it adds to the national product is zero while still adding to such magnitudes. The absolute growth of each of such magnitudes, therefore, is transparently compatible with a continued decline in the welfare of the indigenous population as measured by each and all of the indices suggested above.

(2) The analysis of the first two aspects is confined to mass immigration of non-professional labour with little capital other than personal effects, and in the absence of large-scale *emigration* of similar labour. Provided the excess of immigration over emigration is large, the type of analysis used is relevant. On economic grounds alone immigration of a few thousand or so people a year makes too slight a difference for the country at large to be worth bothering about—though it may have noticeable local effects. The only interesting question for economics is whether a fairly large net inflow of this sort of labour, say, about 50,000 a year or more, has advantages or otherwise for the host country.

---

1 Such as those based on hypothetical over-compensation: E. J. Mishan, 'Recent Debate on Welfare Criteria', *Oxford Economic Papers*, 1965.

(3)   It has been observed from time to time that the economic effects of immigrant labour are comparable with the economic effects of an increase in the indigenous labour force. But even if the effects were identical, restriction of the analysis to immigrant labour alone is warranted on political and administrative grounds. The government cannot as yet directly control the growth of indigenous labour: it can certainly control the entry of immigrant labour. It is to no practical purpose then to argue that importing adult labour is, say, more economical than the domestic production of indigenous labour. They are not, at present, practical alternatives to be decided on efficiency grounds. Total expenditure on children is more aptly regarded as consumption expenditure and, like the annual number of births in this country, can be regarded as determined independently of the immigrant inflow. For the period in question, then, we shall accept the internal population growth as given, the only policy question being whether or not to add to this population growth by immigration, and if so, by how much.

(4)   Any positive role the government might play in attempts to counter or diminish unwanted economic effects of mass immigration is not here integrated into the analysis. There are, of course, any number of precedents for adopting a method that initially abstracts from government policies. Justification for the method is obvious: until there is more information on the direction and magnitude of the effects *in the absence of* government intervention it is not possible to formulate appropriate government policies.

I.   SHORT-RUN EFFECTS: EXCESS DEMAND AND THE BALANCE OF PAYMENTS

(i)   Analysis

One of the manifestations of an 'over-full' employment economy, one subject to creeping inflation, is an apparent over-all shortage of labour. Ministerial remarks in these circumstances that 'we need immigrants for the labour they provide' are transparently fallacious.[1] A country with a labour force larger than that of China can generate this over-all 'labour shortage' simply by adopting policies that result in excess aggregate demand. Although 'over-full' employment, and creeping inflation, may be attributable in the last resort to inept monetary and fiscal management, the question to be answered is whether the import of labour, like the import of goods,

---

[1]   Lord Butler, in replying to the debate on the control of Commonwealth immigration at the Conservative Party Conference of 1961 asserted that we needed Commonwealth immigrants for the labour they provided. The claim has been repeated since by others in high places.

acts to curb the inflationary tendencies by reducing excess aggregate domestic demand. Clearly if immigrants subsisted on hope and fresh air the answer would be affirmative. For they would then add something to the national product and subtract nothing from it. However, they do generate a demand for as well as a supply of domestic goods; and not only a demand for consumption goods but a demand for investment goods also.

In the attempt to determine whether the addition to aggregate demand they generate exceeds or falls short of their aggregate contribution to the domestic product—and, over time, by roughly how much—we shall first consider a 'unit stream' of immigrants; a rate of entry, that is, of one immigrant family per annum. In particular we shall confine ourselves to the Jamaican data, assuming that in each year one additional average Jamaican family enters the country. If we are interested in rough estimates for, say, a constant annual inflow of 50,000 familes, it is necessary only to multiply the unit inflow figures by 50,000.

The magnitude of these aggregates to be traced over this unit time-path are, therefore, quite obviously, (1) The value of the annual *output* over time generated by this unit inflow of migrants, (2) the value of the annual aggregate domestic *demand* it generates over time, and (3) the value of the annual *imports* so generated; all at 1962 prices.[1]

(1) We begin with the information that the average household with a Jamaican-born head consisted, in 1962, of 3.4 persons of whom 2.4 were working, with 1.0 economically inactive or unemployed. The pre-tax earnings of such a household work out at about £1,200[2]— incidentally about 10 per cent higher than the earnings of the average British household in that year, owing to there being a larger proportion of earners in the average Jamaican household. Applying to such earnings an average profit of 26 per cent,[3] the addition to the

---

[1] The economic effects of a unit stream of *emigration* are not, however, symmetrical over time with those of a unit stream of immigration. For one thing, the rate at which capital capacity can be released is limited by the rate of amortisation of the existing capital stock. Thus the rate of additional saving made available by the net outflow of labour differs in general from the rate of additional investment required for a net inflow of labour.

[2] From information based on a survey of seven London boroughs by R.B. Davison. *(Black British,* Oxford University Press, 1966, in particular Table 46.)

[3] Calculated from Tables 1 and 16 in *National Income and Expenditure 1965,* HMSO for the Central Statistical Office, hereafter referred to as the 'Blue Book'.

value of output attributable to each Jamaican household comes to
£1,512.

(2) The time-path of immigrant-generated demand should properly
take account not only of the immigrant family's *initial* expenditure
but, if on balance it exceeds or falls short of its contribution to the
national product, of any subsequent 'multiplier' effects on the
economy. In a full-employment economy any expanding multiplier
effects would take the form of adding to the inflationary impetus,
although initially there could be some period during which stocks
were depleted and queues lengthened. Information about stock and
price responses of industry is much too scanty to warrant specula-
tion about time-lags and the extent of the eventual rise in prices, so
we shall confine ourselves to the initial impact or *primary* demand.
This restriction on the analysis means simply that *if* there is, on
balance, an addition to aggregate demand arising from the unit
inflow, the estimate of *primary* aggregate demand alone is obviously
an under-estimate of the full potential effect. However, since we
are concerned, in the main, with the question whether or not immigration is on balance initially inflationary—something we can
answer—we can afford to put up with a minimum estimate of the full
effects of any excess aggregate demand induced by the immigrants.

The addition to aggregate demand for domestic output arises from
two sources, *current* expenditures and *capital* expenditures. The
former can be divided into three items:

(i)   *current* expenditures out of immigrant's earnings, which is
      equal to earnings after direct taxes, national insurance,
      savings, mortgage repayments, and remittances[1] have been
      deducted;

(ii) *current* expenditures out of profits earned in employing
      immigrant labour after taxes and savings (amounting, in
      1962, to about 77% of profits)[2] have been deducted; and

(iii) *current* expenditure by public authorities for additional
      health and education services, etc., which expenditure is
      deemed to vary roughly with the size of population.

From the total expenditure on finished goods obtained by adding the
figures for the three items, we subtract the average proportion spent

---

[1]   An average of between 10% and 12% of Jamaican earnings goes
      in income tax, national insurance, and personal saving. Remit-
      tances to relatives in Jamaica initially account for between 10%
      and 15% of earnings, though these taper off over time. (Davison,
      op. cit.)

[2]   Estimated from Table 25 of the 'Blue Book'.

on imports, leaving a total that represents current expenditure on domestic goods alone but at *market* prices. By correcting this total to *factor* prices, the effect of all indirect taxes and subsidies is removed from these immigrant-induced current expenditures which turn out to be equal to about 70 per cent of the average immigrant family's gross earnings—or equal to about 55 per cent of the total value of output generated by the immigrant family.

The other source of aggregate demand is the *capital* expenditure needed to accommodate the immigrants in industry and society. The split between social and capital requirements is somewhat arbitrary, though the division between them is of slight importance as compared with the importance of the composite figure. On the assumption that immigrant households have similar requirements to British households we can use the average figure in 1962 of £5,300 of capital per household[1] (excluding import-content and excise taxes), of which roughly one-third would be industrial capital and two-thirds social capital. We have spaced the output response to these capital requirements over two years,[2] so transforming them into annual investment demands.

---

[1] Estimates from data in 'Blue Book', Tables 13 and 61; also from data in P.A. Stone, *Housing & Town Development, Land and Costs*, 1963.

[2] An idea of the method of generating a time-path for a unit stream of immigrants can be conveyed by simple hypothetical data from which economic growth is abstracted. The net domestic expenditure on finished goods generated annually by a single immigrant family entering the host country in year 1 is taken to be 30. The additional domestic value generated annually is taken to be 50. The result of these figures is an excess domestic supply of 20 per annum (written -20). However capital capacity per immigrant family is 200 which we have spaced equally as investment demand over the first two years. Adding 100 per annum for two years to the demand side produces a resultant figure of 80 for the first two years (100-20) and -20 per annum thereafter. In the second year another immigrant family enters and generates exactly the same stream, and similarly in the third and subsequent years. The annual figures for the 1st, 2nd and 3rd families appear in successive lines below, each line beginning one column to the right of the one above.

	year 1	year 2	year 3	year 4	year 5	year 6
1st family	80	80	—20	—20	—20	—20
2nd family		80	80	—20	—20	—20
3rd family			80	80	—20	—20
Time-path for 3 years' immigration only	80	160	140	40	—60	—60

(3) Since expenditures by and on behalf of the immigrants are assumed to have the same import-content as the rest of the population, rough estimates of immigrant-generated imports can be made by reference to the over-all import-content of consumer's expenditure, the import-content of investment expenditure and the import-content of current government expenditure, these being respectively 20, 12 and 9 per cent.[1] Finally, we need to make allowance for immigrants' remittances in order to estimate the additional drain on our balance of payments induced by this unit inflow.

Clearly the estimates of both (2) and (3) above will be critically affected by the expenditures on capital goods since the capital requirements of Jamaican immigrant families are more than four times the value of their annual earnings. The extent to which these capital requirements will result in new investment depends upon the extent of the host country's spare capacity and the distribution of the spare capacity compared, respectively, with the magnitude of the immigrant inflow and its distribution over the country.

If the distribution of the incoming migrants coincided exactly with the distribution of spare capacity, both social and industrial, one could calculate, say, the number of Jamaican immigrant families— roughly 180, 000—that would just suffice to use up an amount of spare capacity represented by 1 per cent of the UK's existing capital stock. Such an exercise might suggest that very little excess capacity is needed to accommodate a sizeable influx of immigrants. However, the little spare capacity that exists in the UK is badly distributed relatively to immigrants' requirements. With respect to social capital, it is to be noticed that, according to the 1961 Census, some three-quarters of Jamaican-born residents settled in the Greater London and West Midlands conurbations where, by standards current in the country, housing accommodation was, and is, scarce.

With regard to the demand for new housing, from the observation that the initial housing requirements of immigrants expend themselves in high rents for over-crowded low-quality accommodation, one cannot infer that immigrants have a small effect on the demand for new

---

If the reader continues the exercise by adding an immigrant family in the fourth and subsequent years, and extends the number of years, he will discover that although all the columns after the first contain two figures of 80 each, the number of negative items (—20) must increase until, in the 11th year, 9 items of —20 exceed 2 of 80, the result being —20. About the turning point from positive to negative, the resulting time-path from adding these columns appears, for the 9th, 10th, 11th, and 12th years, as 20, 0, —20 (calculated in the preceding sentence), and —40 respectively.

[1] Board of Trade, *Input-Output Tables for the UK*, HMSO, 1961.

housing: only that, initially, there is a shortage of housing relative to immigrant requirements (in a country where there was already a shortage even before the immigrant inflow). If it is believed that the government will not allow housing standards to decline and, indeed, will strive to maintain them, sooner or later provision has to be made for additional social capital of a quality comparable to that enjoyed by the rest of the community.

As for the distribution of immigrant workers in industry, although not perhaps as unsatisfactory as the distribution of families in relation to social capital, what is relevant is not merely the excess capacity of industries attempting to absorb immigrants but also the excess capacity in those industries producing goods to meet the initial expenditures generated by immigrants. Since the limited spare capacity in the UK is spread very unevenly over different industries and regions, it is safe to assume that for the relatively large-scale inflow of immigrants—say, 50,000 families per annum or more—by far the larger part of industrial capital requirements, at least within a year or two of the first 'batch' of immigrants, would have to be met from new investment.

(ii) The results

An impression of the likely effects (in terms of 1962 prices) of a unit inflow of Jamaican immigrants on aggregate domestic demand and on imports is conveyed by Table 1 (a) on the assumption that capital requirements are met wholly by new investment, and (b), by way of contrast, on the assumption that capital requirements are met wholly by existing spare capacity—allowing in both cases for a real growth rate per annum of 2½ per cent.

Although it is unlikely that in the first year or two immigrants' capital requirements would be met wholly by new investment, for a constant immigrant inflow of some 50,000 families or thereabouts the (a) assumption is obviously more plausible for the UK in the current economic circumstances than the (b) assumption. Indeed, it is probably more plausible than any alternative assumption. At all events, if all capital requirements have to be met by new investment the excess aggregate (primary) demand generated for a constant inflow of Jamaican-type immigrant families is positive until year 10. Then, and thereafter, a reversal starts, excess aggregate demand being negative. Although no estimates were made of how a rising or declining inflow of immigrants would affect this calculation, it should be obvious that a rising inflow of migrants would tend to lengthen the period of excess aggregate demand while a declining inflow would tend to shorten it.

As for the resulting balance-of-payments series, it will be seen from the Table that whether or not capital requirements are met by new investment, the figure for imports (which includes net remittances

TABLE 1   **Primary Excess Demand and Import Requirements for
an Inflow of one Jamaican Family per Year**

*Assuming that all immigrant capital requirements are
met from:*

Year	(a) New investment		(b) Spare capacity in the existing capital stock	
	Primary excess demand	Imports	Primary excess demand	Imports
	£	£	£	£
1	2,004	687	648	325
2	4,127	1,384	−1,310	645
3	3,598	1,711	−1,985	957
4	3,121	2,035	−2,673	1,259
5	2,623	2,370	−3,375	1,551
6	2,108	2,678	−4,089	1,832
7	1,566	3,000	−4,836	2,126
8	995	3,337	−5,618	2,433
9	395	3,688	−6,436	2,755
10	−236	4,055	−7,291	3,091
11	−899	4,438	−8,185	3,442
12	−1,594	4,838	−9,119	3,809
13	−2,324	5,255	−10,095	4,192
14	−2,089	5,689	−11,113	4,592
15	−3,891	6,142	−12,177	5,009
16	−4,732	6,614	−13,287	5,444

abroad) will increase year by year, though the magnitude will clearly
be larger the more immigrants' capital requirements are met by
new investment—the (a) columns giving the limiting but more realistic
figures for wholly new investment.

It will be observed in the (a) columns that although excess aggregate
demand becomes negative in the 10th year, indicating that then and
thereafter the unit immigrant inflow contributes to excess aggregate
domestic supply, the excess supply is more than offset by the magnitude of corresponding excess imports. This means that the continued
immigrant-induced rise in our international indebtedness, or current excess demand for foreign goods, exceeds the magnitude of the
excess domestic supply from the 10th year onward—the resultant
net imbalance, as indicated in Figure 1, continuing beyond the 16
years covered by the Table.

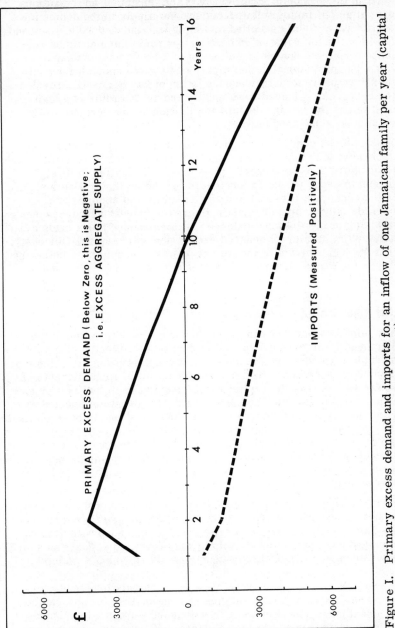

Figure I. Primary excess demand and imports for an inflow of one Jamaican family per year (capital requirements wholly met by investment)

What is the economic significance of this resultant net imbalance over time? If immigrant-induced excess supply in the domestic sector were exactly equalled by immigrant-induced excess demand for imports, the value of domestic resources which could be released from the domestic sector would be *available* for exports (ignoring, provisionally, the import-content of exports), and could therefore prevent further accumulation of foreign debt. Provided the resources released were mobile and substitutible in a high degree and the foreign demand for British goods were infinitely elastic, no more need be said.

Failing these conditions, in particular if the foreign elasticity of demand is less than infinite—and for British goods it is hardly likely to be above 2.5—our export prices must fall relative to foreign prices in order to induce foreigners to take up the available slack in the economy. If export prices do decline, the commodity terms of trade moving against Britain, the real domestic resources needed to maintain international balance will then exceed those made available by the immigrant-induced excess domestic supply. Obviously this is true *a fortiori* if the excess domestic supply falls below the figure for excess imports, as it does during the 16th year and beyond.[1]

(iii) Appraisal of the results

Any mistakes in estimating the behaviour characteristics of the Jamaican immigrant group will, of course, be reflected in the figures in Table I which serve to convey but a rough impression of the magnitudes to be expected from a constant inflow of such migrants. In so far as a part of the capital requirements are in fact met by existing surplus capacity, and in so far as the investment period exceeds two years, the figures in the (a) columns tend to over-estimate the excess (primary) aggregate demand and the excess imports. Yet the critical qualitative results—that over the first decade or so, a constant immigrant inflow will on balance increase aggregate demand in a full-employment economy and add to imports—is hardly open to doubt for several reasons.

First, since no conceivable errors in the estimate of the immigrants' saving or consumption patterns would alter the *qualitative* results of the Table, such qualitative results could be extended with a fairly high degree of confidence to immigrants from India, Pakistan and other economically-backward countries. We could, for example,

---

[1]   Full details of the sources of data, the calculations made, plus a specification of the model constructed for the purpose, can be found in E. J. Mishan and L. Needleman, 'Immigration, Excess Aggregate Demand and the Balance of Payments, *Economica*, May 1966.

double or treble the immigrants' savings propensity, or we could double or halve their receipts of goods and services from the public authorities without being within distance of changing the signs of the figures.

Secondly, we could increase the spread of investment from two years to four or to six years without any alteration of signs and with slight increase in the length of the inflationary period.

Thirdly, although for simplicity as well as realism we have assumed a 100 per cent investment response to immigrants' capital requirements, the shape of the resulting time-path of excess aggregate demand is not so sensitive to error here as may be imagined. Indeed, it can be shown that if only one-fifth of the immigrants' total capital requirements is met by new investment, there will still be some excess aggregate demand until the 10th year. Now one can allow that the proportion of immigrants' capital requirements translated into new investment may be well below 100 per cent, at least in the first year or two. But it is almost inconceivable that—for the size of inflow considered—it will approach a figure below 20 per cent.

Fourthly, after all allowances have been made for possible overestimates of excess aggregate demand and excess imports we may briefly recall certain limitations of the analysis which tend, in contrast, to under-estimate the immigration effects being considered.

In calculating excess aggregate demand the chief limitation has been the restriction to the primary excess demand induced by immigrants. The multiplier repercussions which are explicitly ignored may well be much more powerful than the primary effects estimated. In so far as these multiplier repercussions raise domestic prices relative to foreign prices they cause a shift in the demand from domestic goods to foreign goods, thereby aggravating the deficit in the balance of payments.

Again, our restriction to estimates of immigrant-induced imports under-estimates the resulting balance-of-payments deficiency. Because of a 19 per cent import-content of exports, only £81 out of every £100 worth of goods exported is made up of domestic resources. Thus for every £100 initially imported we have to export an additional £123. The total exports required would, then, have to be about £23 per cent more than the estimate of excess imports in the Table.

Nor can the absence of any estimate of immigrant-induced exports be properly regarded as an omission. So far as I am aware, no economic model, Keynesian, Marshallian, input-output, or any other assumes any direct relationship between national income, or domestic labour supply, and aggregate exports. Exports of the home country, say B, feature simply as the imports of the other trading countries in the model, which imports—like those of country B—are positively related to their national incomes. And the magnitudes of these national incomes are only remotely connected with the number of immigrants entering country B.[1]

Notwithstanding these arguments, there remain two features of the model used which might raise objections: (1) the continued application over time of an unaltered capital-labour ratio in industry, and (2) the assumption of continued neutrality by the government.

Justification for the first, as an approximation, depends upon the length of period in question. Yet even if the real costs of meeting current housing standards, or the standards themselves, fall by as much as a half over the decade the immigrant aggregate demand trends would only be reduced, not reversed. Similar remarks apply to industrial capital.

As for the possible substitution of labour for capital if (in response to the immigrant growth of labour) the wage level tends to fall relative to profits for a period as short as, say, 10 years or so, it is unlikely that the order of magnitude of the fall in relative wages will be such as to encourage the adoption of industrial techniques that are noticeably more labour-using. Be that as it may, the relevance of such an effect in the context of the model, one prone to persistent creeping inflation, and one in which the exchange rate is fixed, is questionable. Wages relative to profits *may* be declining over the period in consequence of the additional immigrant labour, notwithstanding which the initial inflationary impact, which is of major concern here, will continue unabated. Indeed, it is *via* the mechanism of inflation—in which profits rise faster than money wage-rates—that the decline in wages relative to profits is in practice brought about.

The justification for the second feature, the neutrality of the government, has already been indicated. The government can, and in the event of a large and continuous inflow of migrants, should intervene in any of a combination of ways if—as we may suppose—it wishes to combat the resulting inflationary pressures arising from the immigrant-induced excess demand. But whether the response of the government takes the form of larger budget surpluses or tighter money

---

[1] True, if there happens to be some foreign demand for our exports that cannot be met by increasing their output (or raising their prices) because of a sectoral shortage of specialised labour then, provided immigrant labour is able to offer the necessary skills, it can make some temporary contribution to exports. The one industry for which exports could have been increased during the 1960s if the appropriate type of labour could have been recruited was the machine-tool industry. But immigrant labour does not appear to have been used there in any discernible numbers.

or both, success is achieved only by effectively increasing domestic saving in the economy, over the decade, sufficiently to offset the excess of aggregate demand that would otherwise arise. It should, however, be evident that such additional domestic saving brought about by government intervention could, in the absence of immigration, add to the social and industrial capital of the indigenous population.

(iv) Summary

In a fully employed economy, such as that of the UK, in which spare capacity is negligible, a constant stream of relatively unskilled immigrant families has an adverse balance-of-payments effect and, if the stream is large, almost certainly has an inflationary impact on the economy for about a decade (longer if the inflow rises over time, smaller if it falls over time). Thereafter, unless the resulting inflation takes on a momentum of its own, there is apparently an excess aggregate domestic supply. If we could then transfer all the available domestic resources to producing for export, they would not suffice for another decade or so to prevent continued growth of immigrant-induced international indebtedness.

A very rough impression of the order of magnitudes to be expected is indicated by the estimates made for a unit inflow of Jamaican families at 1962 prices, but for reasons given less reliance can be placed on the figures than on their signs. No policy implications follow from this, or any other, analysis. But if the country does choose to add to its growing population by immigration of this sort, it must be prepared for additional pressure on its balance-of-payments and, ultimately, for less favourable terms of trade. The inflationary impact can always be combated by fiscal and monetary policies designed to extract additional saving from the economy—at least, if we ignore possible political difficulties in any further raising of taxes or interest rates.

II. LONG-RUN EFFECTS ON PER CAPITA REAL INCOME AND ITS DISTRIBUTION

(i) Analysis

Over a long period, measured in decades, we may disregard the initial inflationary effects of large-scale net immigration and transform the inevitable adverse balance-of-payments effects resulting from net immigration into adverse terms-of-trade effects—on the assumption that the country seeks over a long period to maintain international balance through a reduction in domestic prices relative to foreign prices. We are thereby enabled to turn our attention to these underlying 'real' effects, from which we can select two indices of economic gain or loss. Over time we trace the impact upon them of large-scale immigration.

Thus A will stand for a measure of the impact of immigration on the distribution of the national product, in particular that between labour and capital, and B will measure the impact of immigration on 'real' per capita income of the *indigenous* population in the host country. A third index, per capita income of the composite population (indigenous plus immigrant), though of general interest in itself, cannot provide a measure of gain or loss to the indigenous population alone. Because of its prominence in policy discussion, however, we shall include it as the C index.

A simple static picture of the economy suggests the sort of answers to expect. Imagine a competitive open economy with fixed amounts of land, capital, and labour. An influx of labour alone (a) will reduce wages relative to profits[1]—the A index falls, the distributional change being 'regressive'; (b), unless there are sufficiently increasing returns to scale, real income per capita of the population as a whole declines—the C index falls; and (c) the real income per capita of the indigenous population rises provided there are no terms-of-trade effects[2]—in that case the B index rises and a gain is registered for the indigenous population. Once we take account of the adverse terms-of-trade movement required to maintain external

---

[1] More accurately, 'rentals', being the market price for the services of capital assets (which could, here, include land), rise relative to the price of unskilled labour.

The returns to skilled or professional labour in the long run partake of the returns to capital—at least in so far as the capital market is such that funds for investment in 'human capital' are available as an alternative to investment in physical capital, or claims thereto.

[2] To be more explicit, the influx of labour causes *wages* (equal to marginal product of labour) to fall more than the average product of labour, and this implies a rise in rentals or a net transfer from wage earnings to profits. However, the part of the transfer as between *indigenous* labour and *indigenous* capital does not matter from the point of view of the *indigenous population as a whole*. We are left then with the transfer from the earnings of the influx of immigrant labour to the profits of indigenous capitalists. Notwithstanding the regressive distributional changes, this additional gain to indigenous capitalists appears as a net gain to the indigenous population as a whole, against which we must set the terms-of-trade effect suffered by both groups of the indigenous population, capitalists and labourers. Dividing this net gain, or loss, by the indigenous population as a whole gives the rise or

balance, however, no clear qualitative result emerges. Estimates have to be made to determine the outcome of the two opposing forces.

The only certain effect emerging from this simple model is the regressive distributional effect, or decline in the *A* index. For *B*, and—once scale effects are introduced—also for *O* there can be off-setting tendencies which cannot be resolved without some idea of the relative magnitudes involved. Estimates of the magnitudes are necessary for another obvious reason: even if the indices are clearly favourable, or clearly adverse, the importance of the contribution economics can make to any immigration policy will depend upon the estimated *magnitude* of the changes induced by immigration.

A somewhat more elaborate model is required, one which traces effects over time in response to a continued inflow of migrants. We shall suppose that a full-employment level of output of the host country is determined, at any point of time, by the existing technical knowledge and by the endowment of labour and capital. Over time, technical knowledge improves steadily—adding, we shall suppose, $1\frac{1}{2}$ per cent per annum to national product for any *unchanged* capital-labour endowment. In the absence of all migration we could estimate the growth in the stock of both capital and labour by extrapolating, respectively, existing net saving and net reproduction rates. This information, along with the allowance of $1\frac{1}{2}$ per cent per annum for improved technology, enables us to trace over time the path of real national income and, therefore, real income per capita (index *C*).

---

fall of its real income *per capita* that results from immigrant labour.

The categories labour (or labourers) and capital (or capitalists) do not, of course, purport to be a description of social realities. They form a convenient economic dichotomy for this kind of analysis and are defined functionally. In so far as an individual's income arises from personal services he contributes as labourer; in so far as it arises from the services of the assets he owns he contributes as capitalist. Most income-earners in Britain contribute to national output in both capacities, as labourer and as capitalist, although most earn the bulk of their income in either one capacity or the other.

The implication for the rest of this essay is that a statement about a transfer or redistribution of income in favour of capitalists is to be interpreted as affecting most people in both capacities, as capitalist and as labourer. If most of his income comes from the services of the assets he owns, he is made better off by the redistribution in favour of capital. If the greater part of his income comes from his personal services, he is made worse off by this sort of redistribution.

With a little more analysis, this time-path will also yield information on distribution (index A) and on indigenous per capita real income (index B). We could then start all over again and trace another such time-path, this time allowing a net inflow of immigrants of, say, 500,000 each year. Observing year by year the differences between the relevant estimates along the two time-paths, we come up with our indices A, B, and C.

Even in so aggregated a model, however, a good deal more information is required than is readily available, or reliable, and the consequent limitations of the method of analysis had better be made explicit before examining the results.

National income for the UK in 1962 was roughly £23,000 million produced with a labour force of about 25½ million—about one worker for every two persons. A rough estimate of average net saving gives it as about 11 per cent of net income. Using a familiar form of the relation between labour, capital, and the resulting aggregate product,[1] to which is added (a) the built-in technological improvement of 1½ per cent per annum,[2] and (b) a 1 per cent increase in the indigenous population over time, we are able to generate a full-employment non-immigration time-path of aggregate real income from which the three indices can all be derived.

Turning to the analogous immigrant time-path we have, arbitrarily, chosen to introduce a constant annual inflow of 500,000 immigrants, *without* additional outside capital, the labour from which is taken to be freely substitutible with indigenous labour. Indeed, for a long-period analysis the assumption is made that, in respect of the average ratio of dependents to earners, the net propensity to reproduce, and the propensities to consume, to import and to pay taxes, the immigrant population is no different from the population as a whole.

In addition to the above assumptions and estimates, there are three critical features of such a model for which dependable estimates

---

[1] One giving a constant elasticity of substitution as between capital and labour, and to which a scale term V may be attached.

[2] More generally, technical innovation can be relatively capital-saving or relatively labour-saving. The more labour-saving an innovation the more it tends to reduce wages relative to rentals. Although on balance, perhaps, labour-saving innovations are more likely over the foreseeable future, the assumption of 'neutral' innovations—those which do not alter the wage/rental ratio—is maintained throughout the analysis. A preponderance of labour-saving innovations over time would act to reduce wages relative to profits. But the distributional effects of immigration would not be much altered thereby.

are not currently available. The first, σ, is the so-called *elasticity of substitution* between labour and capital, and is a measure of the degree to which labour can be substituted for capital. The more elastic is the substitution between capital and labour, the more can labour be used in lieu of capital and the less, therefore, will additional labour tend to depress wages relative to rentals. This elasticity is most frequently taken to be equal to one,[1] which is obviously a convenient figure to work with. Since the results could be sensitive to this value, however, we have made calculations for an elasticity of less than one and more than one. It transpires, however, that the differences made to the indices B and C by changes in this elasticity are not very important.

The second coefficient to which the results might be sensitive is the elasticity of demand in foreign trade, which we need to know in order to calculate the adverse terms-of-trade effect which enters as a negative component into the B and C index. The higher is E_2, the degree of foreigners' response to a reduction of our prices relative to theirs, and the higher is E_1, the degree of our response to a rise in foreign prices relative to our domestic prices, the smaller will be the adverse movements of the terms of trade—brought about, say, by a decline in the value of the pound relative to foreign currencies— necessary to restore international balance.[2] In taking two alternative values for each of these E's of 1.5 and 2.5, we are almost certainly erring on the high side and, therefore, almost certainly under-estimating the adverse terms of trade.

The third coefficient to which the results could be sensitive—and indeed to which the B and C index turn out to be highly sensitive—is V which measures the economies of scale. If when the amounts of both labour and capital are increased by, say, 10 per cent output is increased by exactly 10 per cent V is equal to one and we talk of constant returns to scale. If V were 1.2, a 10 per cent increase of both labour and capital would increase output by about 12. Few economists take V to be much less than 1 notwithstanding that for the country as a whole the amount of land is fixed, but fewer still would adopt a figure for V as high as 1.2. The more common value attributed to V in empirical studies is, not surprisingly, unity, and

---

1 An elasticity of substitution equal to one means that the percentage rise in the amount of labour relative to the fall in the amount of capital is exactly equal to the percentage fall in the price of labour relative to the price of capital.

2 A more complete picture would require also the elasticity of export supply for the UK and abroad. As an approximation we can assume constant costs for the difference in trade made by immigration.

this is the value adopted here. We do, however, make the necessary calculations for a V of 1.2 in order to indicate the substantial difference made to the results by employing such a value.

(ii) The results

The results are tabulated below for selected years from t = 0 (1962) to t = 30 (1992) for three possible cases, each case being a combination of the three sensitive variables mentioned above. Case (1), with the more conservative values of these variables, has estimates of the A, B, C indices for six-yearly intervals, the remaining two cases having estimates only for the first and last years.

Before glancing down the Table the indices will be carefully defined: A, the index of distribution, is defined as the immigrant rental-wage ratio at any point of time as a percentage of the non-immigrant rental-wage ratio. The more this index exceeds unity the more regressive is the immigrant distribution at that point of time compared with the non-immigrant distribution.

B is the increase (positive or negative) of the per capita real income of the indigenous population as a whole as a result of the immigrant inflow up to that year compared with the per capita real income of the indigenous population in the absence of immigration.

C is the increase (positive or negative) of per capita real income for the total population, including immigrants, at any point of time compared with the non-immigrant per capita real income. A positive £ figure implies an immigrant-induced differential rise in per capita real income; a negative £ figure, an immigrant-induced differential fall in per capita real income.

The three cases mentioned above embody the following three alternative combinations of the sensitive coefficients:

Case (1), for $\sigma = 1.0$, $E_1 = E_2 = 1.5$, and V = 1.0.

Case (2), for $\sigma = 1.0$, $E_1 = E_2 = 2.5$, and V = 1.0.

Case (3), for $\sigma = 1.0$, $E_1 = E_2 = 2.5$, and V = 1.2.

In response to a constant 500,000 net immigration per annum over 30 years the indices A, B and C are as shown in Table 2.

An σ above one, indicating greater substitutibility between capital and labour, reduces the positive value of A in all cases and reduces also the negative values of B and C in cases (1) and (2), while increasing the positive values of B and C in case (3) The reverse is true for an σ below one. The only serious difference to the order of magnitudes conveyed by Table 2, however, is in the A index. Thus for an σ of 2 the A index becomes 111 or so for all cases in year 30, while for a σ of 0.5 it becomes about 150 for all cases.

TABLE 2 Indices of Distribution and Increase in Real Income with Net Immigration of 500,000 per year for 30 years

	Year (0 = 1962)	A (in %)	B (in £ at 1962 prices)	C (in £ at 1962 prices)
Case (1)	0	101	−0.83	−1.5
	6	109	−10.42	−14.0
	12	116	−18.50	−24.5
	18	120	−24.76	−35.5
	24	124	−29.33	−47.0
	30	126	−32.30	−54.5
Case (2)	0	101	−0.40	−1.0
	.	.	.	.
	30	126	−11.33	−42.5
Case (3)	0	101	0.90	0.5
	.	.	.	.
	30	123	61.75	17.5

(iii) Appraisal of the results

In view of the somewhat arbitrary, though not implausible, assumptions made, and the parameters adopted as constant over time (such as a constant ratio of earners to population, a constant propensity to save and to import, a fixed net reproduction rate and fixed rate of technological growth), it is unnecessary to stress the tentative nature of the estimates made in Table 2. Nonetheless, despite possible errors in the estimate of these particular parameters, the figures shown are not likely to convey a misleading impression for the simple reason that—although large departures from any, or several, of the above assumptions could result in rather different time-paths than those traced in the Table—it is the *differences* between immigrant and non-immigrant time-paths that enter into our indices *A, B,* and *C.* An alteration in any of the above parameters, would, that is, affect *both* time-paths in much the same way, so that the difference between the resulting immigrant and non-immigrant time-paths is not likely to vary markedly from the magnitudes conveyed by the Table.

There are, on the other hand, the three coefficients mentioned, V (the scale effect), the E's (the elasticities of import demand) and, to a lesser extent σ (the elasticity of substitution), which do bear more directly on the difference between the immigrant time-path and the non-immigrant time-path. Because of the greater sensitivity of the results to these three coefficients, one must take the precaution of experimenting with a range of values for each of them, as indeed has been done in our calculations.

The figure of 500,000 immigrants per annum over a 30-year period may appear high to some people even if it were supposed that the UK resumed its traditional 'open-door' policy at least for Commonwealth immigrants. But the figure in itself is of no importance: the only reason for choosing it is to ensure that the changes wrought in our indices A, B, and C are all large enough to be perceptible. The assumption of a rate of inflow below 500,000 per annum would imply figures (roughly) proportionally smaller than those in the Table, and *vice-versa*.

At all events, the estimates for B and C shown in Table 2 are significant only inasmuch as they are surprisingly small. Those who maintain that immigration imposes large economic losses on the country cannot derive much support from this sort of analysis—not unless they anticipate immigration on a scale very much larger than the 500,000 per annum assumed here. As for those who anticipate economic advantages from net immigration, a case could be made out in terms of the B and C indices only if evidence could be produced of large economies of scale for the country as a whole—of a V larger than 1.2. If, however, the conventional view is allowed to prevail, and for the economy as a whole constant returns to scale are assumed, one must anticipate some decline in over-all real income per capita (indigenous plus immigrant), and some per capita net loss for the indigenous population alone. As suggested above, however, neither is large when taken as a proportion of income per capita or of aggregate income respectively. For an annual migrant inflow of 500,000, for instance, the decline in per capita real income, B or C, does not exceed 6 per cent after 30 years in any of the three cases. This limited decline in per capita real income, B or C, can be attributed in the main to the built-in neutral technological advance that is a feature of our model.

Only for A, the index of distribution, does the outcome look somewhat more sombre. In all three cases immigration makes the resulting income-distribution distinctly more regressive. All three cases, however, assume an σ of unity. If the σ instead were equal to 2, the consequent rise of the A index by 11 per cent over the 30-year period—rentals rising 11 per cent more than wages compared with the position in the absence of net immigration—could be borne with, since real wages would in any case be rising at an average annual rate of about 2 per cent. *Per contra,* if σ were 0.5, there would be a more than 50 per cent rise in the A index over that period which, for the same immigrant numbers, could effectively prevent real wages rising over time, or very nearly.

Is a value of 0.5 for σ at all realistic? There is a tendency today to be impressed with the fixity of proportions in any given state of technology, so that such a value would not be thought implausible. But even if we accept that the proportion of labour and capital is relatively impervious to changes in the prices of labour and capital, we could invoke the opportunities for product-substitution to impart flexibility and limit the relative decline in wages.[1] As suggested above, however, we know practically nothing of the actual size of the consumption effects to be anticipated, and we have no option but to conclude, rather lamely, that the regressive distributional effects of an σ of 0.2 cannot be ruled out on grounds of plausibility.

(iv) Summary

In a long-run aggregative model of the economy in which we ignore all 'temporary' dislocations, all inflationary effects and all external diseconomies, we may plot a movement of three indices, A, B, and C over a 30-year period by comparing an immigrant with a non-immigrant time-path using a number of arbitrary but plausible assumptions for the relatively insensitive parameters while experimenting with the more sensitive ones. Attributing fairly conventional values to the sensitive parameters as in Cases (1) and (2) —σ of 1, V of 1, and E's of 1.5 or 2.5—Table 2 reveals a fairly pronounced regressive distributional effect over time, a decline in the

---

[1] According as wages decline relative to rentals or, what comes to the same thing, as rentals rise relative to wages, more capital-intensive goods rise in price relative to less capital-intensive goods. The greater the response by consumers to such price differentials the more limited is the resulting decline of wages relative to rentals. This substitution on the consumption side acts to reinforce the effects of substitution of labour for capital, so effectively raising the value of σ. No estimates have been made of this so-called *product-substitution* effect and we have disregarded it in the calculations. The larger it is the more it will curb the rise in the index of regressive distribution, A, and the more it will curb the decline in per capita domestic product. If there were no effects on the terms of trade the B index would fall and the C index would rise. Once we allow for the terms-of-trade effects a negative component enters into the B and C index since the relative rise in prices of capital-intensive goods could reduce demand for our exports and add to the adverse movement of the terms of trade. Nevertheless, unless this product-substitution is far more important than is generally believed, our results will not mislead.

B index of per capita income over 30 years of less than £33[1] per annum, and a decline in the *C* index of per capita income of less than £55 in the 30th year. A large enough increase in the economies of scale for the country as a whole—a V of 1.2 or more—would, however, raise both the *B* and *C* index of per capita income to about £62 and £18 per annum respectively. But a value of 1.2 for V would not be regarded by economists as realistic for the country as a whole, and pending evidence contrary to the prevailing belief one may conclude tentatively that an economic case for large-scale immigration, at least one based on indices which would be widely acceptable, is not proven. On the other hand, on the basis of the same indices, the economic case *against* immigration—except on a scale much larger than that conceived in the analysis—is not compelling save perhaps in respect of distributional effects.[2]

III. IMMIGRATION AND 'ESSENTIAL' SERVICES

The popular belief that Commonwealth immigration has helped to overcome shortages in particular service industries may now be examined in an informal way.

It is not always certain, however, that Commonwealth immigrants' entry to an industry suffering from a labour shortage invariably acts to reduce the shortage. If there is among some of the indigenous workers a dislike of working with some kinds of immigrants, or if some stigma comes to be attached to occupations that employ a large proportion of coloured workers, the entry of coloured workers into an occupation can prolong or aggravate the initial shortage of labour in so far as it causes some of the existing workers to leave and in so far as it deters those of the indigenous population who might otherwise have entered. In such circumstances the effectiveness of Commonwealth immigrants in remedying a shortage is reduced and could indeed be negative. The observation of a large proportion of immigrant workers in occupations most easily accessible to them is consistent on this hypothesis with very little increase in total numbers

---

[1] Thus the adverse terms-of-trade necessary to maintain international balance more than offsets the positive transfer to the indigenous population arising from diminishing returns to labour by amounts shown in the *B* column for Cases (1) and (2).

[2] Details of the sources of data and the specification of the model used in deriving these results will be found in the paper by Mishan and Needleman, 'Immigration: Some long-term Economic Consequences' (Part A), *Economia Internazionale*, August 1968.

and possibly with a continuation of the shortage. Public transport[1] and nursing are occupations that might well belong to this category.

Relieving labour shortages by immigration

Allowing, however, that on balance immigrant labour is eventually effective in relieving an initial shortage, is there any clear advantage in following a policy of admitting foreign labour into occupations that are short of labour for the time being rather than adopting the alternative policy of meeting the shortage from existing domestic resources?[2]

(a) *Allocative effect*

Consider first the allocative aspect. To a passenger depending upon a bus or train service, its maintenance at the same fare is understandably preferred to its withdrawal or to its continuance at a higher fare. But this is clearly a partial view only. In the absence of immigrant labour, which may realise this outcome, this sectoral shortage would be remedied in part by a differential rise of wages in public transport. All intra-marginal workers in such an occupation would gain, and this gain must be set against the loss to passengers. A transfer of 'real' income from indigenous passengers

---

1 From 1950 to the present, employees in British Railways and in the London Underground have been declining, as shown by the figures below:

	1950	1955	1960	1965	1968
London Underground	90,000	85,000	77,000	72,000	68,000
British Rail	605,000	563,000	514,000	365,000	317,000

No information about the proportion of coloured workers could be obtained, but it is common knowledge that this proportion has been increasing over this period. What adds plausibility to the hypothesis is a verbal communication from the Public Relations Officer of London Transport that, despite real wages there rising over the period, and at a pace no slower than average real wages in the economy at large, there have been continuing difficulties over the last 15 years in recruiting personnel.

2 We are assuming here that the government is successful in combating inflationary pressure and that there is no apparent over-all excess demand for labour (which, as we showed in I, cannot in any case be met by immigrant labour without further adding to excess aggregate demand). In the circumstances excess demand for domestic labour in some occupations will be offset by a potential redundancy of domestic labour in others.

in favour of indigenous (intra-marginal) workers is the apparent outcome of the non-immigrant solution to the shortage.

But what of the allocative effect? If the shortage in any industry is remedied as effectually by an inflow of labour from abroad as by a release of labour from domestic sources, and if in either case labour moves until the value of its marginal social product is the same in all occupations, then there would be nothing to choose as between the immigrant and the non-immigrant solutions except for two things, one in favour, one against: (i) the non-immigrant solution may take longer, so increasing the loss to the consumers of the service, and (ii) the immigrant solution may imply a lower level of welfare for the indigenous population as a whole as measured by the indices in II—though, as also indicated, such losses as a proportion of the relevant magnitudes are not large. Since these two considerations are opposed in their effects on the indigenous population, quantitative estimates would be necessary to determine the net result. [1]

---

[1] Events that do not fit into the usual framework of formal analysis are nontheless proper subjects for consideration by the economist. In an ideally competitive, frictionless, and informed economy, all the cost-reducing technical innovations are adopted as they appear. The adoption of known labour-saving techniques, on the other hand, takes place in response to a sufficient change of relative factor prices. Thus an influx of additional labour does not of itself *prevent* the adoption of a labour-saving device: the influx must be such as to cause a sufficient rise in the price of capital. Conversely, no reduction of labour in such an economy will of itself encourage the adoption of known cost-reducing labour-saving devices: such devices will appear economical only in response to a sufficient fall in the rate of interest brought about by a reduction in the labour-capital ratio. However, in the partly sheltered and fairly institutionalised economy of the UK these propositions do not hold, except on some definition of 'the long run'. No casual observer of the UK economy would find it hard to believe that some cost-reducing labour-saving innovations are fairly readily available but which, either for institutional reassons (peaceful labour-management relations) or because of the force of inertia, are just not adopted. Without some emergency to act as a catalyst these potential sources of efficiency will be ignored for many years. In transport, for instance, it has long been known that worthwhile economies could have been effected by the employment of one-man buses, by installing coin-operated turnstiles on underground railways, by simplification in fares, and by other labour-saving devices. In hospitals the saving of trained staff by installing patient-monitoring devices in wards is making only very slow headway. It would not be unreasonable

(b) *Long-run consequences*

Let us turn next to the long-run consequences of accepting a policy
of admitting foreign labour to industries claiming to suffer from
a labour shortage. In an advanced and fully-employed economy subject to continual fluctuations in the conditions of demand and supply,
shortages in some sectors are sure to appear from time to time
matched by surpluses in other sectors. The duration of such shortages, and surpluses, will depend *inter alia* on institutional factors
(trade union influences and demarcation rules) and also on the active
policies pursued by governments which bear on unemployment pay,
retraining facilities, incentives to geographical and occupational
mobility, monetary and fiscal management, and so on. A policy of
encouraging immigration whenever a sectional shortage of labour
occurs would, because of its manifest asymmetry,[1] issue in a continued net inflow of foreign labour into the country having the broad
effects discussed in II.[2] However, any rule that sanctioned the admission of immigrant labour into any industry after the persistence of
an unfilled vacancy beyond some agreed time-period might well
lead to increasing friction between management and labour. For
such a rule would clearly act to discourage any employer from nego-
tiating wage increases and providing facilities calculated to attract
domestic labour if, by waiting a little longer, he can meet his requirements by immigrant labour at existing wages.

(c) *'Optimal' population*

Finally, there is the broad question of the so-called 'optimal' size
of population—sometimes identified by economists with a popula-

---

to believe that in the absence of immigrant labour flowing into
these occupations, the apparent shortage of indigenous labour
might have precipitated an emergency in which the provision of
such services could have been met by a change to more efficient,
and already known, labour-saving methods.

1 Symmetry would require that workers redundant in any industry
emigrate from the country.

2 It is sometimes alleged that immigrant labour is 'more mobile'
than indigenous labour. This is certainly true in the obvious
sense that since they came into the country expressly to seek work
they tend to move to areas and into occupations which offer them
employment, whereas the bulk of the existing population is already
employed. In exactly the same sense juvenile and unskilled labour
is also more mobile than domestic labour as a whole. There is
no reason to suppose that as immigrant workers settle down and
acquire skills their mobility will be any better than that of comparable indigenous workers.

tion for which (within a static framework) average product per worker or per capita is highest. As indicated in I, however, there can be no 'economic need' of a larger population or, more precisely, there are no clear economic advantages in Britain either in the short or the long run of a larger population—though landlords and business-men favour a continued growth both for its immediate market-expand-ing effects and for the long-term distributional effects in their favour. If a population larger than that which would result from the growth of the existing domestic population is believed desirable on 'non-economic' grounds—or desirable subject to some restriction on the rate of net immigration—in full awareness of the initially inflationary effects and the long-term regressive distributional effects, then the economist has little to add.

Certainly the so-called optimal population is not an unambiguous economic concept: it can be defined in a number of ways, such as the population yielding the highest per capita income, or the population enjoying the highest over-all level of welfare per family, or that suffering the fewest adverse neighbourhood effects. If an optimum population has any affinity with the latter sort of definition then it is certainly relevant to observe that Britain's population is one of the densest in the world. In particular, the area of England and Wales is today more densely packed with people than either Japan or Belgium. It has about twice the population density of Italy and four times that of France. India, Jamaica, and Pakistan, from where the bulk of the post-war immigrants have arrived, have each less than half the number of people per acre than England and Wales.[1] Holland alone can boast a country more densely populated than ours.

In an era as conscious as is our own of the impending 'population explosion'[2] any proposals for augmenting the already dense and grow-ing population of this country by an influx of people from other lands can no longer depend upon ready acceptance.

IV. EXTERNAL EFFECTS

Some consequences of large-scale immigration do not lend them-selves so easily to measurement as those considered in I and II, but they may be at least as important and a good deal more noticeable. A number of these effects are readily classified as external dis-

---

[1] This information is culled from the *UN Demographic Year Book, 1964*, Tables 1 and 2.

[2] World population today is put at a figure of $3\frac{1}{2}$ thousand million, increasing roughly at the rate of 100 million per annum, by far the larger proportion being contributed by the poorer countries.

economies. In the short run immigrants tend not only to settle in the existing conurbations but, within them, to concentrate their numbers in popular areas or districts, so manifestly aggravating an existing housing shortage and imposing additional burdens on the social services and possibly also on the public transport systems. Inevitably they reduce, for some years, the amenity of the neighbourhoods they settle in.

Social costs of immigration

One can, of course, dismiss such external effects as teething troubles necessarily associated with the process of settling down. Keynes' dictum, that in the long run we are all dead, is relevant in this connection; for it is during the short period in which we live that the discomforts have to be borne with. Such net disutilities as are suffered by segments of the indigenous population are unambiguously a part of the cost of absorbing numbers of immigrants and wherever possible they should, as Pigou puts it, be 'brought into relation with the measuring rod of money'.

(i) *Broad definition*

External effects, however, can be broadly or narrowly defined. On a broad definition any response, positive or negative, of any inhabitant of the host country to the entry of any or each of the immigrants qualifies as an external effect. On such a definition it is not necessary that the economist be able to identify any benefit or damage to an inhabitant arising from the entry of immigrants. The effect can be solely subjective—'pure prejudice', if we like. Without ever meeting a single immigrant the mere knowledge that immigrants, or immigrants of a certain type, are entering the country can add to or subtract from the satisfaction of any member of the host country. On the so-called *Pareto criterion*[1] (which is the foundation of all allocative propositions in economics), unless the gains from immigration can be so distributed as to make every person included in the host population better off, the host country is not to be regarded as better off.[2]

---

[1] Which, in its simplest form, requires that the gains are such that they can more than fully compensate the losers.

[2] No double counting need be involved. Either we could use this test *ab initio,* in which case the benefits of some groups (say, landlords and capitalists), and the losses of other groups (say, workers and pensioners), belonging to the host population are evidently included; else we could summarise these effects in an aggregate net figure such as that given by index B in II. On the assumption that immigrant-induced per capita real income changes have taken place,

On this criterion, then, an economic improvement would require that, irrespective of his prejudices, the sums needed to compensate each member of the indigenous population suffering any discomfort whether 'real' or 'imaginary' from the entry of immigrants could be more than covered by the gains made by other members of the indigenous population *plus* the gains made by the immigrants.

(ii) *Narrow definition*

A narrower definition of external effects, one I favour,[1] would exclude all those responses to others' behaviour that cannot count on an almost unanimous approval of the society in question. Thus evidence of direct damage to a man's property, or health, or physical environment, or peace and quiet would, in Britain I think, be almost universally regarded as relevant to the issue. Dissatisfaction arising solely from private principles or prejudices would, however, not qualify as agenda on this narrower view.

If we accept the narrower definition of external effects, the ideal experiment is then to determine for each locality into which immigrants enter, or affect by the repercussions they generate, the minimum sum (reckoned either as a capital sum or annual payments) which (if received by the affected members of the indigenous population on condition of admitting into the localities in question a known number and type of immigrants) would in practice make the members indifferent as between receiving the immigrants and maintaining the *status quo*.

Needless to remark, no one has yet attempted to estimate the magnitude of these compensatory payments, and while this is no reason for failing to mention them, or for failing to dwell on them,[2] it must be admitted that there is no firm basis even for a guess at the social costs involved.[3] For the present, then, no more can be done

---

however, we could go on to measure the external effects only and place them on a per capita basis. The algebraic sum of these two has to be positive for a per capita over-all benefit to be established.

[1] For reasons set out in the first three chapters of my *Welfare Economics: An Assessment,* North-Holland, 1969.

[2] For it is not impossible that if somehow these external effects could be brought into the calculus they would completely swamp any evaluation of the economic effects treated in I and II.

[3] The possibility of immigration in large numbers creating factionalism and discord within the community, or of their forming disruptive power-groups within the host country, are consequences

than explicitly to acknowledge their incidence and potential significance, and to offer the obvious generalisation that they are likely
to increase with the number of immigrants, their rate of arrival,
their initial level of poverty and lack of sophistication, and with the
degree of their concentration within already densely populated areas.

V. CONCLUSION

In conclusion one may hazard a prediction. With the inevitable extension of communications there will follow, among the economically
under-privileged, an acute awareness of the increasing disparity between their standards of living and those of the ordinary workers
in economically advanced countries. In the *absence* of government
checks to immigration, the growing temptation to migrate to the
few prosperous countries open to them would be strengthened by
private shipping and airline companies which would find it profitable
to encourage mass migration by offering cheap passenger rates
and credit facilities. As it is, and even in the presence of government controls, one can reasonably anticipate a growth in the numbers of illegal immigrants into the wealthier countries, in particular
into Britain and North America.

We are not, however, precluded by the above observation from making attempts to ameliorate the economic conditions of the poorer
countries if we conceive it to be part of our moral duty to do so.
Though some proponents of liberal dogma appear reluctant to concede the possibility, an economic policy may yet be acceptable to
the nation without necessarily redounding to its material advantage.
If, therefore, on moral grounds we wish to make some contribution
to the well-being of the poorer countries we could make our contribution the more effective by undertaking a careful examination
of the various methods of affording economic relief (such as re-
moving trade barriers to their sales of products in this country)
and by giving direct aid as an alternative to the policy of transfer-
ring some part of their growing populations to these already crowded
islands.

Considerations of distributional justice would seem to favour exporting capital rather than importing populations. We should hardly
regard it as fair to earmark the additional capital sent abroad—
which would be an alternative to using it to equip immigrants entering Britain—to be distributed among those families that might other-

---

which formally can be comprehended by the concept of external
effects. But since the range of likely consequences is better
brought to the fore by harnessing the experience, specialised
knowledge and judgement of the whole community, it is more satisfactory to try to reach a consensus by the democratic process.

wise have entered this country. Rather we should want our aid distributed within the poorer country according to some more acceptable principle of social priorities. As an alternative to the export of capital, the import into Britain of a small proportion of their populations is, then, a highly unsatisfactory method of distributing economic relief to poor countries. As a means of promoting economic advance in such countries this alternative is also less efficient on allocative grounds.

6. THE POLITICAL ECONOMY OF IMMIGRATION CONTROL

GRAHAM HALLETT
University College, Cardiff

THE AUTHOR

Dr. Graham Hallett, who studied Philosophy, Politics and Economics
at University College, Oxford, has held University posts in Canada,
West Germany and Cambridge, England; he is at present a Lecturer
in Economics at University College, Cardiff. He began his academic
career in agricultural economics, publishing two books on agricultural policy, *The Economics of Agricultural Land Tenure*, Land Books
Hutchinson, 1960, and *The Economics of Agricultural Policy*, Basil
Blackwell, 1968, and was joint author (with Gwyn James) of Hobart
Paper 22, *Farming for Consumers*, published by the Institute of
Economic Affairs in 1963. He later worked in various fields of
economics. He has a special interest in urban problems; he is pre-
paring a text-book on the subject and will shortly publish a report
on ports and industry in South Wales.

I. GENERAL CONSIDERATIONS

Preliminary comments

At the present time, questions of immigration and race relations
are highly controversial, or at least touch a number of raw nerves.
A writer risks offending people if he goes beyond abstract principles,
such as that we are all children of God (and even this, the Rev Ian
Paisley told Mr James Callaghan, is a highly erroneous statement).

Thus an economist who examines these questions faces a dilemma.
Should he try to confine himself to 'objective' facts and analysis,
excluding value-judgements, or should he make his value-judgements
quite explicit? This is a question examined by Professor Gunnar
Myrdal in his classic study of the race problem in the USA.[1] His conclusion is that complete objectivity is probably impossible: one's
value-judgements are likely to influence, for example, the kind of question one examines. The best course is to make one's value-judgements explicit, so that readers can take account of them. This view
is not shared by all social scientists, but it is one to which I sub-
scribe. Although it is highly desirable to examine migration questions in a factual, analytical manner, we ought to recognise that
value-judgements are inextricably involved; in most cases, academics
who purport to be purely scientific either have nothing useful to say
or have unconsciously incorporated value-judgements into their
analysis.

Moreover, it is undesirable to consider merely the narrowly 'economic' aspects, in the sense of the effect on the national income. Professor J. K. Galbraith and others have criticised the predominant
importance often attached to a few per cent either way in the annual
rise in real national income. The effect of immigration on social
relations and the 'quality of life' is more important. Some economists, while accepting this principle, maintain that on grounds of
division of labour they should confine themselves to the effect of immigration on national income, and leave it to others to take the more
intangible factors into account. But a self-denying ordinance by
economists inevitably leads to a very one-sided view of the subject,
while the general public, and even economists themselves, are in-
clined to forget that it *is* a one-sided view. A feeling has thus arisen
that, in general, economists need to take a broader view than they

---

[1] Gunnar Myrdal, *An American Dilemma*, Harper & Row, New
York, 1944, Introduction, 2.

have done recently, to learn from other disciplines; and recover something of the broad, commonsense approach of the earlier 'political economists'.

The history of international migration

Why do people migrate? The earliest long-distance migrations had physical causes, and involved large groups; thus the mass migrations of the Goths, Vandals and other tribes into Europe towards the end of the Roman Empire, which resulted in so much confusion, were caused by the drying up of grazing grounds in Central Asia. In the modern era (meaning since the 16th century) long-distance migration has consisted of movement from one nation to another; has generally been undertaken by individuals or small groups; and has been inspired either by the desire to escape political or religious persecution, to seek a 'better life' in some non-economic sense, or to obtain a higher economic standard of living. The largest movement was from Europe to the Americas between the 16th and 19th centuries, rising to a peak in the half century before the First World War. This was the heyday of international migration, when over 50 million people migrated, predominantly from Europe to the Americas. As Professor Brinley Thomas has shown,[1] this movement was paralleled by capital movements, which provided the infra-structure in the relatively empty receiving countries. This combined movement of capital and labour to countries with plentiful land but relatively little labour and capital was of considerable benefit in their economic development. It also benefited the European countries through the production of cheap food and raw materials that it made possible. Thus it was the satisfactory kind of arrangement in which both sides benefited.

This gain was, at least, true of the temperate, fairly empty countries such as the USA, Canada and Argentina. It was probably also true of the tropical countries with long-established populations, such as India and Malaya, where the immigrants consisted of small numbers of skilled personnel who organised administration and various forms of plantation production. It has been fashionable in the post-war period to denounce colonial 'exploitation', but it now seems doubtful whether—at least in British colonialism—there really was exploitation, in the sense of harm to the economic development of the colonised countries. It is true that the British, as colonisers, did not push industrial development. But they did nothing to stop it—as they had done in Ireland or the American colonies under the influence of Mercantilist economics in the 17th century. And in the light of the

---

[1]   Brinley Thomas, *Migration and Economic Growth: A Study of Great Britain and the Atlantic Economy,* Cambridge University Press, 1954 (new edition forthcoming).

often disappointing progress with industrialisation made by the ex-colonies since independence, it may be doubted whether more rapid industrialisation at an earlier period would have been wise. It is now clear that an infra-structure of transport, civil administration and education is the prerequisite for industrialisation, and this the British as colonisers provided to an astonishing degree.

Apart from the emigration from Europe, there was also the move-ment of a million Indians to less heavily populated parts of the Empire, notably East and South Africa and what is now Guyana. The Indians played an important role in the development of these coun-tries, but in the light of what is now happening it is interesting to note how this immigration was regarded at the time. To quote one book on the subject,

> 'The sociological problems which would ultimately arise if Indians did begin to settle in the colonies in large numbers, were lightly held in the early years of immigration'.[1]

Since the First World War, considerable changes have occurred in population movements. There has been a reversion to the practice—last implemented in the Dark Ages—of killing or expelling whole minority populations (Armenians in Turkey, Jews and Germans in Eastern Europe, Indians in East Africa, Ibos in Northern Nigeria, etc.). But apart from these forced migrations there has been sub-stantial migration since the Second World War, although on a smaller scale than before 1914, and of a somewhat different charac-ter. It has taken the form predominantly of a migration from less developed to more developed countries, and can be divided into two categories: a movement of unskilled labour from less developed countries to Western Europe, and a movement from all over the world of skilled labour (the 'brain drain') to Western Europe and, more importantly, the USA. There has been some movement of un-skilled labour from Turkey, Greece and other Mediterranean coun-tries to West Germany and Switzerland, although mainly on tem-porary residence and work permits. The more important—because more lasting and less assimilable—migration has been from the Indian sub-continent and the West Indies to the UK. On the other hand, the movement of skilled labour, particularly doctors, has been to the USA, from both the under-developed countries and Western Europe. In the UK, there has been a 'musical chairs' type of migra-tion with doctors migrating to the USA and doctors from India and Pakistan taking their places. This has been brought about by differing immigration restrictions in the USA and UK.

---

[1] I. M. Cumpston, *Indians Overseas in British Territories 1834-1854,* OUP, 1953.

Both skilled and unskilled immigration has given rise to concern, although broadly speaking it is the receiving countries that have been concerned about the immigration of unskilled persons, and the sending countries that have been concerned about the emigration of skilled persons. The fear in receiving countries has been of *Überfremdung,* whereas the countries suffering from a 'brain drain'—whether the UK or India—have been afraid they would suffer economic harm.

In economic terms, these population movements can be thought of as an example of the tendency for a factor of production, such as labour, to move to where the return is highest. This applies within a country, where there is a tendency for people to move out of regions or occupations with relatively low incomes into more prosperous regions or occupations. This intra-national movement will—like water in a series of tubes finding a common level—tend to cause a levelling out of income differences. However, because of various 'frictions', such as attachment to an area and a social circle, the movement is often slow, and not sufficient to eliminate income differences between regions. The frictions restraining movement between countries—differences in language and ways of life—are normally much stronger than between regions of the same country. In addition, international population movement is often restricted by controls on immigration, and occasionally on emigration.

Immigration and morality

Are there any absolute moral or economic imperatives in international migration? It is generally accepted in Western countries that people should be free to move within a country (in Communist countries movement often requires official permission). Should countries which believe in freedom for its citizens to move within its boundaries allow free entry to citizens of other countries? Or should those who believe in free trade and the market economy logically support free international movement of people? Both arguments have been made.

There is a significant difference between population movement inside a country and movement into it from the rest of the world. Movement within a country does not affect the total population of the country; moreover, there is generally a similarity in ways of life between people in one country. This is often not so with immigration, although some immigrants will be more alien than others. Immigration controls are imposed to deal with the economic and social problems resulting from a rise in total numbers, or the special problems arising from the influx of people of a different race, religion or cultural background. If these problems are genuine, there is a case in principle for immigration control, whatever may be said about its detailed application. The question is whether these problems are genuine, or whether, as is often alleged, they are founded on prejudice.

'Prejudice'

It is necessary to say something about the word 'prejudice', which recurs frequently in this context. It is often difficult to know what meaning to attach to it, since it is often used in a sense beyond that of a pre-conceived, incorrect opinion. As Professor Ruth Glass, a sociologist, writes:

> 'Prejudice can be described as a negative, conspicuous, hostile or contemptuous attitude towards a group as a group—an attitude which is usually associated with the assumption of that group's inferiority'.[1]

When this sort of definition is used as the basis for empirical work, the results are sometimes open to objection. For example, *Colour and Citizenship*[2] gives the results of a survey of 'colour prejudice' in the UK, and the finding that 'only 10 per cent of the population is prejudiced' was widely publicised. The questionnaire used for the survey was not given in full, but included such questions as whether there should be controls on coloured immigration, whether immigrants should be given council houses, or whether Indians, Pakistanis or West Indians 'take more out of the country than they put into it'. This survey raised some controversy of a technical kind. A correspondent to *New Society* (21 August, 1969) calculated that the proportion classified as 'prejudiced' or 'prejudice-inclined' in one sample could be raised from 13 per cent to 43 per cent by altering the weighting of the questions. No one seems to have asked what a question like 'Do the Indians take more out of the country than they put into it?' *means*: that their economic contribution has not brought about a rise in real average national income? That the disadvantages—social, political and economic—of having the Indian community outweigh the advantages? That the net effect on the balance of payments is negative? These are complex and difficult questions, and it does not seem obvious that anyone who answers 'Yes' rather than 'No' is prejudiced. The question is probably merely designed to elucidate 'attitudes'. But if so, do the percentage answers of a single survey possess the scientific validity claimed for them?

---

1 Ruth Glass, *Newcomers: The West Indians in London,* Centre for Urban Studies, 1960, Introduction.

2 By E. J. B. Rose and others, Oxford University Press for the Institute of Race Relations, 1969, Ch. 28.

The basic moral question is whether it is inherently wrong to refuse
to allow a man to make his home in any country he wishes, in the
way that most people would accept the absolute character of 'Thou
shalt not kill' (although even this Commandment is subject to qualification by all except pacifists). No country in the world has in
recent times allowed completely unrestricted immigration, and virtually no one has proposed it for the UK. Even those who most
strongly opposed the 1962 Commonwealth Immigration Act wished
to maintain free entry only for citizens of Commonwealth countries—for Indians, but not Indonesians, for Nigerians but not Nor-
wegians—and did not advocate similar rights for all human beings.
The argument could hardly, therefore, be said to be based on universal human rights.

II. PRINCIPLES

Immigration and economic theory

Must immigration control be ruled out by a liberal economic philosophy? Can free movement of population be justified on the same
grounds as free trade between countries? Some economists maintain that it is in the interest of a country to allow free imports of
goods even if other countries do not reciprocate; does the same
apply to movements of people?

We are, of course, a long way from free international trade in goods
and capital, and economic arguments can be made for all kinds of
restrictions. Any general economic pronouncement—such as that
free trade is good or bad—has to be based on an economic model
simpler than the infinitely complex reality. On given assumptions—
such as that there are stocks of resources in the various countries
which will be used in the most profitable way—it can be shown that
free trade is beneficial for the world as a whole, or even for an individual country, if it is not large enough to influence the terms on
which it trades.[1] But when complicating factors are introduced
the stark simplicity of the prescription vanishes. Perfectly valid
arguments for restricting international trade can be adduced on
grounds of defence, economic development, the well-being of social
groups, and much else.

Does it follow, as is often said, that free trade has been discredited?
By no means. One can still argue that free trade is likely to be
preferable to any other system: that departure from it is a self-
perpetuating process which leads to intensifying bureaucratic control over the individual, even to the point where the state restricts

---

[1] C. T. Kindleberger, *International Economics*, Irwin, Third Edition,
1963, Parts II and III.

the right to travel abroad; that the best policy is therefore free trade. Or, at a more modest level, one can advocate more freedom in the foreign exchange market than the citizens of many countries—including the UK—possess at the moment; I would certainly do so. But one cannot say 'economics proves' that any departure from free trade is inevitably harmful.[1]

If this is the somewhat agnostic position of economic theory on international movement in goods, the position is still less conclusive on movement of people. After all, the inflow of a few million Japanese transistors raises fewer problems than the inflow of a few million Japanese. Some economists have constructed theories based on the concept of nations having given stocks of labour and capital (the Heckscher-Ohlin approach, in its original form).[2] This theory was mainly intended to explain international trade, but it was sometimes used for conclusions regarding migration, such as that free movement of labour would allow a better 'mix' of capital and labour.

International movement of goods can, however, to some extent be regarded as an alternative to movement of factors of production, that is, labour and capital. There has been an unprofitable debate among economists on whether trade can be a complete substitute for factor movements. The conclusion in an exhaustive study by Professor J. E. Meade is that trade will be a complete substitute for factor movements only under particular conditions.[3] Free trade may have to be accompanied by free factor movements if total production in the international economy is to be maximised, although this conclusion is based on very static and restrictive assumptions. But Professor Meade adds two arguments in favour of controls in two cases: when there is a rapid rise in population in the 'sending' country or when welfare policies differ markedly between countries. On the basis of experience over the last hundred years, one could perhaps make the more general point that, except in virtually 'empty' countries, free population movement is feasible only when there is similarity in the cultural, social and economic status of the sending and receiving countries. Thus free movement of labour is possible

1 This point is made, in an unnecessarily obscure way, in I. M. D. Little, *A Critique of Welfare Economics*, 1950, Ch. XIII: 'Welfare Theory and International Trade'.

2 J. Bhagwati, 'The Pure Theory of International Trade: A Survey', in *Surveys of Economic Theory*, Vol. II: *Growth and Development*, American Economic Association and Royal Economic Society, 1967. For a summary, see P. T. Ellsworth, *The International Economy*, 3rd edn., Chs. 4 and 5.

3 *The Theory of International Economic Development*, Vol. II: *Trade & Welfare*, O.U.P., 1955, Chs. XIX-XXII.

in the EEC because there are now no wide disparities between the
member countries. The pressure of Italian emigration has been
considerably reduced by Italian economic growth in recent years,
but Italy still presents some problems to other member countries.
Free movement of population has remained possible between the
UK and the Republic of Ireland, but the free movement of population
that existed between the UK and India in the 1950s proved not to be
feasible.

To return to economic theory. The traditional Heckscher-Ohlin
theory of international trade is based on a rather over-simplified
division of resources into land, labour, and capital: this became
clear when Professor W. Leontieff tried to verify the theory empi-
rically, and came up with such curious results that even economists
realised that something must be wrong.[1] A recent survey[2] makes
the point that it is inappropriate to think simply in terms of 'capital'
and undifferentiated 'labour'. The skills and knowledge possessed
by labour—sometimes referred to as 'human capital'[3]—are what is
important in a modern economy. (This conclusion may seem fairly
obvious to non-specialists, but it is good to know that it is taken into
account by economic theorists who, in their quest for a neat, co-
herent explanation, are prone to omit from their theories relevant
factors appreciated sooner by 'practical' men.) This changed approach of economic theory makes it even more difficult to lay down
any simple rule about the economic effects of the migration of unskilled labour, not to mention the social, cultural and economic implications. As Professor Howard S. Ellis points out[4], the income
effect of migration has been reduced. Today a rise in real incomes
depends far more on improvements in 'know-how' and the supply of
appropriate investment than on the level of labour supply.[5]

[1] W. Leontieff, 'Domestic Production and Foreign Trade: the
American Capital Position Re-examined', *Economia Internazionale*
Vol. 7, 1954.

[2] H. G. Johnson, *Comparative Cost and Commercial Policy Theory
for a Developing World Economy,* Wicksell Lectures for 1968,
Almquist & Wiksell, Stockholm, 1968.

[3] G. S. Becker, *Human Capital,* New York, 1964.

[4] 'Are there preferable alternatives to international migration as
an aid to economic development?', in Brinley Thomas (ed.),
Economics of International Migration, 1958. (Proceedings of a
Conference held by the International Economic Association).

[5] For a short summary, C. P. Kindleberger, *International Economics,*
Ch. 22: also *Europe's Post-War Growth: the Rule of Labour
Supply,* 1967, which lays considerable, perhaps excessive, empha-
sis on labour supply.

We conclude that neither ethics nor economic theory can tell us anything about the *principle* of immigration control. We simply have to study what happens: the experience of other countries, the problems of the particular country's economy, its density of population, the potential number of immigrants, the ease or otherwise with which they fit into their new country, and the administrative arrangements in operation. The argument has to be a pragmatic one about the likely results of various policies rather than a theological debate or a slanging match.

Emigration

Before leaving general principles, a word on the other side of the coin—emigration. In the age of Mercantilism in the 17th century many states prevented their citizens from emigrating because they feared economic harm to the nation. This policy has been revived by totalitarian governments in the 20th century. Citizens of Communist countries are not allowed to emigrate without permission, and attempted emigration is a serious offence (except in Cuba, which has deliberately allowed most of its former professional class to emigrate). Even in Western countries, concern has been aroused at the exodus of skilled personnel, mainly to the USA. A study of the emigration of doctors from the UK estimated that between 1955 and 1962 British doctors left at the rate of 392 per year, equivalent to about a quarter of the output of British medical schools.[1] There is some evidence that the exodus has increased in recent years. There is less information on other professional and technical groups, but there seems to have been a substantial outflow.[2]

The question of whether emigration is economically harmful (and, if it is, the secondary question of what policies should be adopted) has recently been the subject of academic debate. One of the most valuable controversies has been reprinted in the Penguin Readings,[3] and a variety of viewpoints are represented in an excellent recent symposium on the 'brain drain'.[4] On the level of 'positive' economics, the issue at debate is whether emigration from a country harms those who do not emigrate. One view seeks to use welfare

---

[1] B. Abel-Smith and K. Gales, *British Doctors at Home and Abroad*, G. Bell, London, 1964.

[2] Brinley Thomas, 'The International Circulation of Human Capital', *Minerva*, Vol. V., No. 4, Summer 1967, reprinted in M. Blaug (ed.) *Economics of Education 2*, Penguin Modern Economics Readings, Penguin Books, 1969, pp. 250-280.

[3] *Ibid.*

[4] Walter D. Adams (ed.), *The Brain Drain*, Collier-Macmillan, 1968.

economics to argue that emigration is unlikely to inflict substantial harm on the rest of the nation.[1] The argument is that employees may be expected to be paid the value of their marginal product and, therefore, their emigration will harm the rest of the nation only if there are either market imperfections which cause them to be paid less than their marginal product, or externalities which cause their contribution to the general welfare to exceed the services paid for through the market. It is then argued that externalities and imperfections are likely to be small, so that emigration does little harm. Against this view, it has been argued by Professor Brinley Thomas that externalities and imperfections are often considerable, and that large-scale emigration of skilled persons may do considerable harm, especially to developing countries who have so few skilled people, but even to countries like the UK.

I find unconvincing the *a priori* argument that emigration cannot possibly harm a country, and would accept that it could in some circumstances be harmful. But even if this view is accepted, there is the further question of what the response to emigration should be. This raises issues of a more 'normative' kind. Some economists, among whom one of the most distinguished is Professor H. G. Johnson, take a very internationalist or cosmopolitan approach, arguing that all that matters is the well-being of the individual, and that it is morally wrong to think in terms of *national* well-being.[2] At the other extreme are those who pay little attention to the individual, and think of education primarily as an investment by the state, from which the state is entitled to obtain a return, even if this means forbidding individuals to emigrate. This approach, carried to its logical conclusion, has produced the 'Socialist protective wall' in Berlin.

In between these two extremes is a middle ground represented, with variations of emphasis, by Professor Brinley Thomas,[3] Professor H. Myint,[4] and Professors W. D. Adams and J. B. Dirlam.[4] They argue that the nation cannot be ignored in economic policy, but that individual wishes also have a very high priority, and that the freedom of the individual to leave his own country must be preserved. However, emigration is often the result of frustration with the prevailing system: 'the brain drain phenomenon has a vital message, especially for the "losing" nations: the fault lies not only in your

---

[1]   H. G. Grubel and A. D. Scott, 'The International Flow of Human Capital', in *Economics of Education 2, op. cit.*

[2]   'Criticisms of Thomas's Analysis of Brain Drain', in *Economics of Education 2, op. cit.*, pp. 281-290.

[3]   *Op. cit.*

[4]   Contributions to *The Brain Drain, op. cit.*

stars, but also in you'. The response should therefore be to modify the institutions or financial distortions which contribute to the brain drain, whether in career structures, the financing of higher education, or taxation.

Granted that we cannot say that it is inherently wrong to control immigration, can we say that it is inherently wrong to control emigration? I believe that we can, without being inconsistent. The economic and social consequence are by no means comparable. If a country opens its frontiers to a much larger country—say, the UK with 50 million and India with 500 million—the number of immigrants can be a large proportion of the population of the receiving country. But except when there is natural catastrophe (the Potato Famine), or an extremely repressive government (German Democratic Republic), there has never, in modern times, been a huge exodus of people from a country; most people's attachment to their surroundings is too strong. On the other hand, if a significant number of people 'vote with their feet', this is usually an indication that something is wrong, and a good way of bringing pressure to bear on the authorities to remedy it. I would suggest that, although there ought to be no right of immigration for citizens of other countries, there ought to be a right to emigrate.

III. HISTORICAL CONSEQUENCES

Multi-racial societies

On the consequences of immigration, unless we make the highly questionable assumption that social processes are quite different in the UK from elsewhere, the UK can learn a good deal from the history of other countries. Immigrations of people of different race, religion or culture have occurred in most countries, on a small or a large scale. Sometimes the peoples have lived together in peace, sometimes not. The first conclusion that can be drawn is that numbers, both nationally and locally, are crucial. In most countries, small numbers of immigrants have been absorbed without difficulty, whether, as in the UK they are completely assimilated, like the Huguenots; assimilated while retaining their group identity, like the Jews; or remain unassimilated, like most Chinese. But this type of integration implies splitting up local concentrations of immigrants, and their acceptance of the ways of life of the host society. When the proportion of immigrants rises above a certain level, the situation changes. Small numbers of Jews had lived in reasonable amity with Arabs in Palestine up till the First World War: with the rise of the Jewish population thereafter, the situation changed dramatically.

A study of countries in which immigration of different races, nationalities or religions has produced mixed populations, suggests three types of result. First, a melting-pot in which inter-marriage has brought about a new amalgam. This has, with some important exceptions, occurred in the USA and Latin America. In the USA, the various European nationalities have to all intents been blended; the main group remaining unassimilated is the black population. In Latin America there has been a considerable amount of inter-marriage over the three centuries since the Spanish conquest, probably more than in any other part of the world. But this process has not gone so far as to eliminate completely race problems in Latin America. The British Royal Commission on Population (1949) argued that a systematic policy of immigration could be welcomed without reserve only if the immigrants were not prevented by religion or race from inter-marrying with the host population, and merging with it. This policy—one with distasteful overtones and based on colonialist attitudes, according to *Colour and Citizenship*[1] —was not however implemented in the 1950s.

The second situation is that of communities which remain distinct, in a state of latent antagonism, at times breaking out into violence. This is broadly the situation between blacks and whites in the USA, blacks and Indians in Guyana, Chinese and Malays in Malaysia and Indonesia, Hindus and Moslems in India, Greeks and Turks in Cyprus, Protestants and Catholics in Ulster.

The third situation is of distinct communities establishing a peaceful working relationship, based on a 'pluralistic' system. There are not many examples, and most of them are based on geographical separation. The most successful is probably Switzerland. Canada has attempted the same approach with its English-and French-speaking communities; it will probably succeed, although it is perhaps too soon to judge. In both these countries, the communities were of European origin and so had a good deal in common. It is hard to find a system of this type embracing different races in the modern world, although it may have existed in India or the Middle East in past centuries. In the USA, recent developments in relations between black and white point more in the direction of a federation of communities than of assimilation. The more extreme black leaders have non-plussed the old supporters of 'integration' by demanding racial segregation and black states. Even apart from these extreme demands, some of the more promising developments have been in the self-government of black town districts in matters such as education.

Developments in the USA are of particular interest because the UK has a habit of following developments there about 15 years later. The American Negroes were originally concentrated in the Southern States; but mechanisation reduced the demand for agricultural

---

[1] *Op. cit.*, p. 208.

labour, while the industrial development of the South lagged behind that of the North (minimum wage laws being perhaps a contributory factor). This caused a migration to the cities of the northern USA. The black people settled in the older central areas, which were being abandoned by the whites seeking more space and greenery in the suburbs, and the influx of blacks triggered off an accelerated exodus of whites. Thus was created the 'black ghetto'.

The way in which West Indians and Indians and Pakistanis have settled in London, Birmingham and some northern cities since the early 1950s has been similar to the sequence in the USA. Immigrants have settled in the poorer, central areas of large cities, and some of the indigenous population has moved out so that districts with a high proportion of immigrants have been formed. They are smaller and often less rigidly defined than in American cities, but they have very similar characteristics, as a study of one area in Birmingham makes clear.[1]

Elementary micro-economic market theory explains the sequence. The settlement of immigrants in a district leads to some inhabitants putting their houses on the market, and so to a fall in house prices. As more immigrants move in, a split market develops with house prices lower for sale to whites than to immigrants. When the area becomes predominantly immigrant, a new market is established, for immigrants only. Prices tend to be high by comparison with houses of similar quality elsewhere, because the immigrant area is restricted, and the settlement of immigrants in other areas is discouraged by public authorities as well as individual action. *Colour and Citizenship* uses an expression from the American literature: the 'noose' of white suburban areas surrounding the ghetto.

Housing in the ghettoes, in both the USA and the UK, is not always bad and overcrowded. The Los Angeles black suburb of Watts, scene of one of the worst riots of recent years, does not have 'bad housing'. The density is low, the housing sound—and deadly dull. Ghetto housing is, however, frequently overcrowded, bad and dear. This seems to be the outcome of several factors. There is severe pressure on the available housing of ill-informed consumers in a weak bargaining position. Reputable landlords tend to move out with the influx of immigrants, leaving property in the hands of less reputable landlords (often immigrants). In the UK, the whole situation has been aggravated by rent control. The housing problems of the ghettoes are in part the general problems of the central areas of cities, which have been increased by immigration.

It may be government policy to encourage dispersal from the

---

1   John Rex and Robert Moore, *Race, Community and Conflict,* Oxford University Press, 1967.

ghettoes: one cannot be sure. In any event, it is not taking place very fast. Clearly much needs to be done to relieve the problems of education and community relations in immigrant areas, but it is hard to deny that these problems will be intensified by further coloured immigration, which in the first instance affects the existing immigrant population.

The impact of coloured immigration has thus been mostly on working-class people, rather than on the medium- to high-income group, which includes those engaged on intellectual work who have produced most of the literature on immigration. Until recently, it has been the supporters of Afro-Asian immigration who have made the running in the press and broadcasting, and who have frequently chosen to castigate the 'poor whites'. More recently, a few voices have been raised suggesting that—to take an extreme case—a TV personality who has just bought a £ 90,000 house in Belgravia is perhaps not the best person to pillory a working-class man worried about the effect of coloured immigration on his district. *Colour and Citizenship* rejects this view:

> '...nothing can excuse the disgraceful way in which the liberals are now being treated. ...In fact, there is good evidence to show that the middle class intellectuals have more contact with the ordinary immigrant than the working class in whose name they are ritually belaboured.'[1]

The survey of attitudes is cited in evidence, although no evidence pointing to such a conclusion is in fact presented.

There is, of course, as Mr Rose and his co-authors mention, considerable ambiguity about the term 'liberal'. The classical liberalism of J.S. Mill was concerned with freedom in society for individuals and groups, but the term has recently been applied to persons holding views which must make J.S. Mill turn in his grave—such as enforced state monopoly in education, or the right violently to suppress differing views. In the context of *Colour and Citizenship*, the term appears to mean those who opposed restrictions on Commonwealth immigration. My own view of the 'liberals' differs from that of Mr Rose, for I should have thought that a good deal of 'ritual belabouring', or worse, had come from their side; one rarely reads of advocates of unrestricted Commonwealth immigration being howled down at universities. But our law-makers, while paying lip-service to the 'liberals', have in practice decisively rejected their views. The outcome of this schizophrenic stance has been a lack of serious discussion on legislation. More robust—but good-tempered and courteous—controversy on coloured immigration at

---

[1]   *Op. cit.*, p. 12.

an early date might have led to better thought-out legislation than the 1962 and 1968 Acts.

Post-war immigration into the UK

The legal arrangements under which the Indians and West Indians came to the UK were part of the decline and fall of the British Empire. Under the Empire there had been—in theory more than in practice—free movement of population within an Empire, because everyone was a subject of the King-Emperor. After the War, the Empire was transformed into the 'British Commonwealth of Nations' (as some people mistakenly still call it: the 'British' was quietly dropped in the 1950s). During this transitional period, the 1947 Commonwealth Citizenship Act allowed any citizen of the independent countries of the Commonwealth to enter, and settle in, the UK. When large numbers of immigrants from Africa, Asia and the West Indies took advantage of this privilege, it became obvious to the authorities that serious social problems were spreading, and that immigration would have to be restricted. But the 1962 Commonwealth Immigration Act was essentially a holding operation, which added basically inconsistent provisions to the Commonwealth Citizenship Act of 1947, without modifying it. The 1962 Act was opposed by the Labour Party and by many intellectuals on the ground that there should be unrestricted free entry for citizens of other Commonwealth countries.

When faced shortly afterwards with the responsibility of office, the Labour Government became a passionate supporter of the 1962 Act. It then raised incomparably more serious constitutional issues by passing the 1968 Commonwealth Immigration Act, which restricted entry not only of citizens of independent Commonwealth countries but even of the Asians and whites who had been offered the choice of UK or Kenyan citizenship when Kenya became independent and had chosen UK citizenship. We shall return later to these unfortunate people, but will first examine the whole argument for and against immigration.

'Coloured immigration'

Before going into the argument for and against immigration, we must face the truth that the kind of immigration that has created difficulties is not from Australia or Canada or New Zealand but from India, Pakistan, Africa and the West Indies, in a word, Afro-Asian, or coloured, immigration. But there has been a reluctance to mention the fact, or even to refer to colour, based on a laudable desire to avoid emotive terminology, and to stress that there is no 'colour bar' in UK society. But it has unfortunate consequences. Skin colour is one of a person's characteristics—together with hair colour, dress, behaviour, temperament, and physique. Moreover, colour is associated with race, and so often with temperament and in many cases with cultural background. These obvious characteristics apply, of course, to 'whites' or pinks, as well as to blacks, browns or yellows: we all have a colour of some sort. Let us by all means avoid terminology that causes offence, but we need words to describe facts.

The recent report by the Institute of Race Relations[1] argues that we ought not to be afraid to mention the existence of colour. This is sensible, although the further proposal—tentatively supported by a Select Committee of MPs[2]—that 'records be kept which distinguish employees by ethnic origin'[3]—is more questionable. It will be ironic if, in the pursuit of non-discrimination, the same methods are used in the UK as have been used in Nazi Germany or South Africa in pursuit of discrimination.

For purposes of policy on Commonwealth immigration, the important distinction is not colour as such, but between Canada, Australia, and New Zealand on the one hand, and Africa, the West Indies, India and Pakistan on the other. There are wide differences of culture and temperament between the peoples of the latter countries, but they have in common that they are 'underdeveloped'—with corresponding unemployment and low income levels—and that the number of potential immigrants (especially from India and Pakistan) is large in relation to the population of the UK. Quite apart from questions of language, religion and culture (for the Indians and Pakistanis) and colour, their economic and demographic condition put them into a different category from Australia, New Zealand and Canada. The present arrangements for admission to the UK of citizens of all Commonwealth countries are extremely unsatisfactory and cause needless unpleasantness. I shall outline some proposals for reform at the end of this essay.

The history of recent immigration

Why did the influx take place in the late 1950s? Did it indicate that the UK needed these immigrants? It was argued in the 1950s—and is still accepted by many—that, since the immigrants came because of a demand for their labour, the immigration was in everyone's interest.

---

[1] *Colour and Citizenship, op. cit.*

[2] *Report from the Select Committee on Race Relations and Immigration: The Problems of Coloured School-leavers,* Vol. 1, HMSO, 1969, pp. 57-8.

[3] *Colour and Citizenship, op. cit.,* p. 711

As far as can be judged, immigration did arise from a demand for labour. In the inter-war period, the high level of unemployment meant that there was no demand for immigrant labour, while in the immediate post-war period immigration was hindered by controls. In the 1950s the UK entered into a phase in which there were shortages of labour in some sectors of industry and government. Moreover communications had improved, so that the news that there were jobs in British cities spread quickly to the West Indies and even the Indian sub-continent.[1]

The types of jobs filled by immigrants from Asian, African and West Indian countries can be divided into three main groups, raising diverse issues. There were skilled occupations, notably doctors, nursing, and miscellaneous unskilled work. The doctors, coming mainly from India and Pakistan, illustrate a phenomenon seen on a much larger scale in the USA in recent years—the brain drain of highly skilled professional people from the undeveloped to the developed countries. It arose mainly because the planners of British post-war medical policy (notably the Willinck Committee) under-estimated the demand for doctors and made inadequate provision for medical schools. In addition, the hierarchical organisation of British hospitals and the pre-occupation of the BMA with general practioners resulted in the pay of junior hospital doctors being low, and conditions of work bad. Thus the UK experienced a shortage of hospital doctors, and newly-qualified doctors from India and Pakistan found openings which, even if pay and conditions were poor by British standards, were good in comparison with what they could obtain at home. Over one-third of the doctors now in British hospitals come from the developing countries, and there has been a net flow of doctors from under-developed countries to the UK.

Nursing, on the other hand, is an occupation which, in all developed countries, is finding difficulty in attracting sufficient recruits. Poor pay—resulting partly from enforcement of British incomes policies only against occupations that do not strike—may have been a contributory factor. But there is likely to have been a shortage in any case.

In unskilled labour, the shortage arose from the loss of attraction of unskilled jobs or with full employment and a wider range of job opportunities, while automation and mechanisation had not yet developed to the point at which many of these jobs could be done by machines. The normal effect of a shortage of labour would be to raise wages. At first wages remained low because these occupations had traditionally been regarded as low-wage; later, wages remained low because of the increased supply of immigrant labour. Holding

---

1   C. Peach, *West Indian Migration to Britain*, Institute of Race Relations, 1968.

down wages in lower-paid jobs was in 1961 and 1962 considered desirable by the Treasury, which opposed the Commonwealth Immigration Bill on the ground that immigration helped to maintain the current incomes policy. A somewhat contradictory argument,[1] made admittedly mainly with Australia in mind, is that the temporary pressure on resources caused by the immigrants' needs for housing and other forms of investment may cause inflation. A sharp increase in immigration will, in the short run, raise the demand for housing and other forms of investment proportionately more than the rise in population: this may give rise to inflationary pressure in the short run. In a British context, it is probably truer to say that it will cause pressure on accommodation in immigrant areas.

IV ARGUMENTS FOR AND AGAINST

The arguments for either welcoming or controlling coloured immigration can be divided into the narrowly economic and those raising broader social and political issues. The economic arguments can be further divided according to whether one is considering the advantages and disadvantages to the 'receiving' or 'sending' countries.

(i) *'Labour shortage' argument*

In discussing the economic arguments, it is first necessary to make some points which might have seemed so obvious as not to deserve mention, had they not been overlooked in popular discussion, government publications and even academic debate. At certain phases in the trade cycle of a developed economy, 'labour shortage' arises. But this type of shortage is not the kind which can be corrected by importing more labour, in the way that a shortage of potatoes can be cured by importing more potatoes. It is a reflection of demand inflation, arising from 'too much money chasing too few goods', and can be dealt with only by fiscal or monetary policy. There is also the universal post-1945 problem of creeping 'cost inflation' arising from the monopoly power of trade unions, and no one has yet discovered how to deal with it.

The notion that 'labour shortage' can be corrected by importing more labour ignores the difficulty that labour is people, who consume as well as produce. If the aim (or, rather, one aim) of economic policy is to raise real income per capita, rather than merely total national income, there is no advantage to the host country in importing more labour if it increases national income in proportion to the number of immigrants. The only case for immigration—from

---

[1] W. M. Corden, 'The Economic Limits to Population Increase', *Economic Record,* November 1955.

the narrowly economic point of view of the host country—is if it raises significantly the average per capita real income of the whole population. Except perhaps in the case of a country with a very sparse population—hardly the British case—there is no such thing as a *general* shortage of labour, which can be cured by importing more labour; immigration can be relevant only to shortages of *particular kinds* of labour.

This error was one of the many that arose in the ill-fated 'National Plan 1965-70'. The planners asked industries how much labour they would need in 1970, on the assumption that national income would rise at a faster rate than anyone thought it would. Having got these figures—which as we now know were drawn out of the air—and adjusted them in various ways, the planners added them up and compared the total with the forecast total of the labour force in 1970. [1] They found that the forecast demand was 200,000 more than the forecast force.[2] Now anyone who knows anything about the official statistics of what happened five years ago, let alone the projections of what is going to happen five years hence, will appreciate that a margin of 200,000 on a labour force of 20 million—an error of 1 per cent—is to all intents spot on. However, several economic commentators seized on this 'manpower gap' as a justification for immigration, thus compounding statistical and theoretical confusion.

It is true that, in a penetrating article,[3] Professor R.C.O. Mathews spoke of an 'increase in the scarcity of labour relative to capital'. But by this he meant an increase in the amount of capital per worker and the virtual elimination of the pool of casual or under-employed labour coming off the land typical of 19th-century England and many under-developed countries today. This change by no means implies the need to tap the reserves of unskilled labour in the under-developed countries. Indeed, on Professor Mathews' analysis, this policy would tend to restore the 19th-century type of 'structural' unemployment, which would probably increase price stability but would be very objectionable in other ways.

(ii) *The 'helot' argument*

The simplest argument for immigration is that immigrants are needed to do the low-paid or unpleasant jobs that the indigenous population is no longer prepared to do. We will term this the 'helot'

---

1 John Brunner, *The National Plan,* Eaton Paper 4, Fourth Edition, Institute of Economic Affairs, 1969.

2 *The National Plan,* Cmnd. 2764, HMSO, 1965, p. 35, para. 20.

3 'Why has Britain had full employment since the War?', *Economic Journal,* September 1968.

argument: it is the familiar argument that without immigrants the National Hospital Service, transport, etc., would collapse.

The immigration of the 1950s appears to have occurred because of shortages of labour. But if the immigrants who take these jobs are to be allowed to remain permanently in the country, there are two inferences: either this type of labour will—at best—last only as long as the working life of the original immigrants, or their children will remain in an inferior social group, prepared or forced to take work that white people will not accept. The latter was obviously not the wish of those who advocated immigration on 'labour-shortage' grounds, and most people would like to see immigrants, and especially their children, being given an equal start compared with everyone else. There is thus an inherent contradiction in the argument that, on the one hand, coloured immigration benefits the domestic population by giving it 'an up-grading in the occupational hierarchy'[1]—that is, the 'helot' argument that the coloureds can do the low-paid jobs—and, on the other hand, that there must be no discrimination, and that the law should be invoked to ensure that there is a representative proportion of immigrants at all levels of employment.[2] My own view is that the 'up-grading' approach is both socially objectionable and economically unsound.

There is considerable evidence, from more advanced economies than the UK's, that much of the demand for unskilled labour experienced by Britain in the 1950s was a transient phenomenon. North America, in particular, has found that mechanisation and automation eliminates many of these jobs very rapidly, with the result that unskilled labour becomes a drug on the market. The unemployment problem in North America has for many years been primarily that of the unskilled. In Canada, many men who once earned good money in heavy physical work find their muscles no longer needed. In the USA, the problem coincides to some extent with that of colour: the Negroes in the northern 'ghettoes'—quite apart from discrimination in employment—are difficult to employ because of their low level of education and training, which results from the social and educational situation in the ghettoes. It is now a serious problem in American economic policy that the black unemployment rate is higher than the white, but moves with it. If the Nixon administration's attempts to curb inflation result in the unemployment rate rising to, say, 4 per cent, the rate among the black population will be nearer 8 per cent, and substantially higher in some districts, or among teenagers.

The decline in demand for immigrant labour will not be universal. In some occupations or industries which received immigrants, such

---

[1] *Colour and Citizenship,* p. 655.

[2] *Colour and Citizenship,* p. 711.

as nursing, the demand for labour is not likely to decline; but the availability of immigrants reduces the incentive to make changes which would have tended to attract more indigenous labour. The normal reaction to a shortage of labour is a rise in wage-rates, even though it may take some time for employers' attitudes to change. If jobs such as dustmen or junior hospital doctors have traditionally been regarded as low-paid, a shortage may last some time before the employers realise that they will have to pay relatively high rates. In the UK the availability of immigrant labour has probably made it easier for the National Health Service to continue paying low salaries to junior hospital doctors and nurses and perpetuating conditions which drive doctors to emigrate. It is possible that—especially with nurses—there might have been shortages in any case; but better pay and conditions usually increase supply. At present, British hospitals would collapse without Indian and Pakistani doctors, but it is highly questionable whether allowing this state of affairs to arise has been in the interests of either Britain or India and Pakistan.

The immigration of people with special skills may nevertheless sometimes be beneficial. In countries which lack an entrepreneurial tradition, the immigration of small numbers of skilled men who integrate with the local population can be of appreciable benefit, for example, in many countries of Asia and Africa.[1] In many instances, however—such as the Indians in Africa and the Chinese in S.E. Asia—enterprising immigrants do not integrate with the indigenous population: they consequently become unpopular and are often expelled or, in extreme cases (e.g. the Chinese in Indonesia), are massacred. Britain has probably benefited in the post-war period from the settlement and integration into the community of small numbers of men with skills lacking in the local population. In my opinion, we could still do with a few German railwaymen in the administration of British Rail and more Italian restaurateurs. But this type of small-scale immigration is quite different from large-scale immigration. We return to the question of numbers.

(iii) *Balance of payments argument*

Immigration may have an effect on a country's balance of payments because of the remittances made by first-generation immigrants. This could be offset if immigrants made exceptionally small purchases of imported goods, which is highly unlikely, or if they made an exceptionally high contribution to exports, which is rather unlikely. The net effect on the balance of payments is therefore likely to be negative. This is not, of course, bad. It is a form of aid

---

1 T. W. Silcock, 'Migration problems in the Far East', in Brinley Thomas (ed.), *Economics of International Migration, op. cit.*, Ch. 18.

to poor countries, possibly a more useful form than aid through governments. And in a country with a chronic tendency to surplus, like West Germany, it is a means of reducing the surplus. This is hardly a problem likely to be faced by the UK in the longer run.

(iv) *The 'expanding industry' argument*

A somewhat more sophisticated version of the 'helot' argument for immigration has been presented by some economists.[1] It is that the expansion of new branches of industry, on which economic progress depends, is likely to be held up by labour shortages because of the immobility of labour moving out of declining industries, especially when they are situated in other parts of the country—coal, steel, etc. An inflow of labour enables the new industries to expand without a corresponding decline in the old.

The first question to ask is whether the expansion of newer industries is in practice hindered by shortages of unskilled labour. There is little evidence that this is true. The constraint on the expansion of new, modern industries is nearly always the supply of skilled, rather than unskilled, labour. The appropriate policy would therefore seem to lie in education and industrial training. The requirements of a modern economy in which techniques are rapidly changing is that as many people as possible should be given a basic training, which provides the basis for further specialisation, while retraining facilities should be available so that new skills can be taught when necessary. The important input in a technological economy is not labour, pure and simple, but the modern skills that are combined with it.

From this point of view, British performance has been chequered. It is only since the Industrial Training Act that an attempt has been made to set up a universal system of industrial training such as Germany has had for a century. An alternative to immigration would have been more re-training facilities for redundant workers in declining industries: and for these workers at least there is no doubt which policy is preferable.

The economic arguments for large-scale immigration which we have considered are thus extremely short term. They concentrate on short-term advantages, and ignore the problems being piled up for the future. They are based on the kind of economics of which Professor P.J.O. Wiles has well written:

'Keynes switched our attention to the short run. Not only good but also great harm has followed ... a certain demoralisation

---

[1] E.g., Professor Maurice Peston, in *Colour and Citizenship, op. cit.* Ch. 31.

has also set in, a certain slick irresponsibility, an exaltation of immediate convenience over permanent duty, a neglect of the coming generations. ... In the long run we may all be dead, but our children are all alive.'[1]

(v) *Social and cultural arguments*

On the social and cultural effects of immigration, arguments can also be adduced on both sides. In favour of immigration it can be argued that Indian restaurants, West Indian jazz, Asiatic dignity and African exuberance all increase the richness of the otherwise somewhat drab British cultural scene. It is also argued that the presence of Afro-Asian immigrants gives Britain the opportunity to establish a 'multi-racial society' thus giving a lead to the world, and establishing a link with the 'Third World'.

As against these arguments, large-scale immigration of racially distinct peoples into a settled country has usually caused conflict. Moreover, there is little evidence that large-scale immigration from developing countries improves relations with them. Australia openly and Canada implicity restrict immigration predominantly to Europeans, but their relations with the 'Third World' are in some ways better than the UK's.

The social consequences of immigration depend on the degree of integration achieved. Integration was originally used in the sense of amalgamation or assimilation, so that colour was irrelevant. All the evidence is that it can be achieved only as the result of extensive inter-marriage, which in the case of black and white means a large coffee-coloured population. A coffee-coloured race would probably be admirable, but other multi-racial societies indicate that its growth would be very slow. More recently, there has therefore been a tendency for integration to be defined in terms of *modus vivendi*[2] rather than of its original meaning of assimilation. In purely visual terms, Indians and Pakistanis—who will soon be by far the largest immigrant group in the UK—would be more easily assimilated in a white society than black people. But in this case there is a strong tradition of racial/cultural/religious exclusiveness, as exemplified in the history of Indian communities in East Africa and elsewhere.

(vi) *The 'colonial debt'*

A further argument for coloured immigration, that the UK is under a moral obligation to the ex-colonial countries to admit their citizens, can be resolved into three questions. Does Britain have an obligation to help the under-developed Commonwealth countries,

---

1 *Price, Cost and Output,* Oxford, 1961, p. 294.

2 *Colour and Citizenship*, p. 514.

either because of colonial exploitation, or on other grounds? If it does, is immigration in the interests of these countries? If it is, should help be given in this way?

The argument from colonial exploitation raises the fundamental question whether any nation owes reparation to another for the wrongs done by its ancestors to the ancestors of the present citizens of the other country. It is by no means self-evident that it does, especially as most nations have been beastly to most others at some time in their history. My judgement is that a country has a limited obligation to another country so long as the sins of its ancestors still adversely affect conditions of life in the 'wronged' country. If this test is applied to the countries of Asia and Africa which were once British colonies, it is not at all apparent that the colonial experience has left them worse off than they would otherwise have been. It is, of course, difficult to speculate on what might have been, but a comparison of Jamaica with Haiti, or Ghana with Liberia (or the record of Hong Kong's industrial success), does not suggest that the ex-colonies would have been much better off if they had never been under British rule. This is not to defend Britain's post-colonial follies 'East of Suez', but one should be fair about that historical curiosity, the British Empire.

I would suggest that Britain has no obligation at all to Pakistan, India, and the African states on the grounds of past colonial exploitation. The case is somewhat different for nations which are the outcome of the slave trade, notably the West Indies, or even for minorities which are the descendants of indentured Indian workers who (albeit voluntarily) moved to other parts of the Empire, notably Kenya, South Africa and Guyana. For these people, I would judge that Britain still does have some obligation originating in the past (and especially to East African Asians who were offered UK citizenship quite recently). There remains the different argument that Britain, like other developed countries, has an obligation to help the under-developed countries, just because she is richer than they are. I would agree that Britain does have a moral obligation to render *useful* aid to the under-developed countries, although it should be emphasised that their fate rests for the most part in their own hands.

Does emigration benefit the under-developed countries?

The further question arises: Is immigration to the UK in the interests of the 'sending' countries? It may be said that it must at least be in the interests of the immigrants who come to the UK, since they have revealed their preference in the most obvious way. But the interests of those who remain in the homeland cannot be ignored. It can be argued that the sending countries suffer from rising populations (which is denied by economists such as Colin Clark but accepted by most) and that emigration relieves this pressure. In

relation to the total population increases in the under-developed
Commonwealth countries, the amount of relief provided by migration
to the UK is insignificant. Between 1950 and 1962, approximately
one million people migrated from the under-developed Commonwealth countries to the UK; during the same period, the population
of India and Pakistan alone rose by 75 million. It is, therefore, clear
that migration to the UK can have no significant impact on the
population problems of the under-developed Commonwealth countries
as a whole. This was true even in the 19th century.

> 'International migration, even in the heyday, could not do much
> to alleviate population pressure: it produced its beneficient
> results through marginal adjustments in particular areas.'[1]

It would seem, therefore, that the immigration of the 1950s and early
1960s was, in aggregate, of no significant benefit to the under-
developed countries of the Commonwealth. Against the benefits from
remittances sent home from the UK must be set the effect of the
losses of some skilled or more enterprising workers, but in any
case the impact is trivial in relation to these huge populations. On
the other hand, immigration has caused problems in the UK which
should not be exaggerated but are by no means negligible.

V. SUMMARY OF UK IMMIGRATION STATISTICS

Numbers of immigrants in the UK

There are at present roughly $1\frac{1}{4}$ million recent coloured immigrants in the UK. The number of immigrants seeking work has been
cut sharply from 28,000 in 1963 to a mere 5,000 in 1967. But the
number of relatives, who at present are allowed to join anyone in
this country, remained at around 50,000 a year until it dropped to
28,000 in 1969. A parliamentary answer in the summer of 1968 (based
on the Registrar-General's estimates) stated that by 1985 there
would be $3\frac{1}{2}$ million immigrants or descendants of immigrants in
the UK. Later in the year a Government spokesman suggested that
this figure was an over-estimate because it assumed the continuance
of present fertility rates, and that a more likely figure was $2\frac{1}{2}$
million.

A detailed study has recently been published in *Colour and Citizenship*. This takes the immigrants from India, Pakistan, the Caribbean
and West Africa, who in 1966 totalled 848,100. It is estimated that
this number will rise to 2,074,000-2,373,000 by 1986. Among the

---

[1] Brinley Thomas, *International migration and economic development*, UNESCO, 1961, pp. 42-3.

various groups, the most striking change is the quadrupling of the
Indian and Pakistani group because of their high fertility. The pro-
jection assumes that immigration of wives and children will continue, totalling in all 121, 000, including 95, 000 children.[1] This may
be an under-estimate, since a recent report by a House of Commons
Select Committee calculates that over the next ten years 250, 000
child immigrants of all ages will have been admitted.[2] Both estimates (95, 000 or 250, 000 children) are based on calculations by
Mr David Eversly and Mr Fred Sukdeo.[3] The rather large difference
between Mr Rose's estimate and that of the Select Committee arises
from different assumptions on the proportion of relatives who will
come to the UK.

It therefore seems certain that by 1986 the UK will have a coloured
population of from 2 to $2\frac{1}{2}$ million. And unless there is some
sudden change, which experience in this country and others gives no
reason to expect, most of this population will be concentrated in
urban areas, including the present immigrant districts. Thus the
'ghetto' seems likely to remain with the UK for a long time. Under
the circumstances, continued restriction on coloured immigration—
as distinct from visits—seems justifiable from all points of view.

**Estimated Future UK Population of Major Immigrant Groups,
1966-1986**

Country of Origin	1966	1986 (low fertility projection)	1986 (high fertility projection)
India	223, 600	768, 000	890, 000
Pakistan	119, 700	408, 000	485, 000
Caribbean	454, 000	815, 000	904, 000
West Africa	50, 800	83, 000	94, 000
Total	848, 100	2, 074, 000	2, 373, 000

Source: *Colour and Citizenship*, Table 30.1, p. 633.

[1] *Colour and Citizenship, op. cit.*, Appendix Table VIIIi.

[2] Report from the Select Committee on Race Relations and Immigration, *The Problems of Coloured School Leavers*, vol. 1, HMSO,
1969, p. 10, para. 22.

[3] *The Coloured Population of England and Wales and their Dependents*, Institute of Race Relations, Special Series, 1969.

VI. CONCLUSIONS

British immigration policy

There is still a wide range of views on immigration policy. At one extreme there are those who, like the Bishop of Stepney, would welcome 10 million coloured immigrants as a means of 'bringing fresh blood into a tired old country'.[1] At the other extreme are those who would wish to emulate the Kenyan or Ugandan policy towards ethnic minorities. In between are a large and increasing number of people who have come to feel that there is a need to control immigration, especially mass immigration from densely populated Afro-Asian countries. Of course, having acquired a race problem in a fit of absent-mindedness, the UK must do what it can to solve it. It may be possible to do so in a relatively short period, by comparison with other countries, perhaps two or three generations. But it would be unwise to intensify it by allowing further large-scale coloured immigration. This at least is the general view, and academics are slowly coming round to accepting it.

The basic issue of immigration control is in every sense academic, since the principle has been accepted by both main political parties, and will clearly not be abandoned. But it is important that intellectuals who opposed the 1962 Act, and have since quietly regarded it as a deplorable sop to the 'poor whites', should reconsider the basic issue, and conceive whether they might possibly have been mistaken. Because many leader writers, academic economists and broadcasters have regarded the generally accepted principle of immigration control with contempt, they have been unable to give any serious consideration to its detailed operation. Thus the proposal to alter the unsatisfactory position of temporary visitors from Commonwealth countries by putting them on a par with aliens has received little serious discussion.

The most pressing need is to make it possible to issue residence permits of limited duration to nationals of other Commonwealth countries. Such a person can be refused admission to the UK, but if he once enters it (or at least stays more than 28 days) he can legally remain here for the rest of his life. This means that any professed visitors are subject to suspicious and unpleasant interrogations, for the very good reason that, if they turn out not to be *bona fide,* they cannot be deported. This has already caused unnecessary unpleasantness to a number of visitors, and friction with both India and New Zealand. If Commonwealth citizens were on a par with aliens, it would be possible to issue short-term residence permits for visitors, longer-term permits for students, and permits on a different basis for settlement.

---

[1] Debate with Mr Enoch Powell, ITV, 11 October, 1969.

Proposals on these lines are made by Mr E. J. B. Rose and his co-authors in *Colour and Citizenship,* which marks an abandonment of the 'liberal' policy of unrestricted Commonwealth immigration. *The Economist,*[1] still apparently unwilling to concede that there can be honest differences of opinion on this question, gave a cynical explanation: 'even professional liberals are affected by the political climate on as tricky a subject as this one'. Although not always agreeing with them, I prefer to believe that Mr Rose and his colleagues have been led to their conclusions by the logic of the facts. In any event, the support of the Institute of Race Relations' study is an encouragement to honest discussion. The proposal is not new,[2] and has been attacked on two main grounds: (a) that it was 'racist' and anti-Commonwealth; (b) that the existing arrangements provided for a tighter control on Commonwealth citizens than on aliens. The support of *Colour and Citizenship* makes it more difficult to apply at least the first of these two arguments. The present system is one which no government would ever have devised as such. It arose because a measure of a holding type (the 1962 Commonwealth Immigration Act) was grafted onto an Act based on incompatible principles (the 1947 Commonwealth Citizenship Act) without a re-drafting of the whole law. The time is now ripe for a re-drafting of this legislative mess.

'Limited residence' or reciprocity?

Residence permits for limited periods would put an end to most of the unpleasantness that characterises visits to the UK by Commonwealth citizens. But this would have to be accompanied by a revised definition of British citizenship. The Conservative Party proposes that Commonwealth citizens should be treated in the same way as citizens of other countries, who can apply for citizenship after five years' residence. It is certainly hard—given the state of the Commonwealth—to justify preferential arrangements for Commonwealth immigrants as such. But some Commonwealth countries—notably Canada, Australia and New Zealand—give preference to British citizens, which are not at present being reciprocated. British citizens are welcomed in Canada or New Zealand, but the citizens of these countries are treated by the UK in the same way as citizens of countries which certainly do not welcome British settlers. Is there not a case in equity as well as self-interest for reciprocity? Canada, for example, welcomes British immigrants and allows them to acquire Canadian citizenship, if they wish, without the normal waiting period. Should not the UK reciprocate?

---

[1] 12 July, 1969, p. 26.

[2] It was contained in the Conservative Party's progress report, *Mak Life Better,* 1968.

I would also suggest that free trade in people is easiest when the disparities between the countries are not too wide: in levels of income, economic development and unemployment, and in race and culture. This reciprocal free movement is possible with Ireland, and in effect exists; it would be possible with Canada, Australia and New Zealand; it would be more difficult with the West Indies, and much more difficult still with India and Pakistan. It has sometimes been suggested[1] that the same restrictions on immigration should apply to Irish as to Indians. I would argue, on the other hand, that more 'Irish'-type arrangements are desirable, provided of course that they are acceptable to both countries.

The system I would advocate is similar to that in force in Canada, Sweden, West Germany, or the USA. Residence permits of different kinds would be available; permission to stay for short visits would be readily available; so would permission to stay for periods of several years for *bona fide* study; permission to take up employment would, with exceptions, be restricted to skilled persons who had already been engaged by an employer, or to citizens of countries with which the UK had entered into reciprocal arrangements. For Canada, Australia and New Zealand this would merely require that the UK reciprocated the preferences she at present receives from them. It might be possible to make comparable arrangements with other European countries, quite apart from the reciprocity involved in possible Common Market membership.

Two forms of citizenship

It is frequently argued that the type of reform advocated by *Colour and Citizenship*, and the Conservatives, would make the present Commonwealth immigrants in the UK feel insecure, and drive them into the arms of Black Power.[2] It is hard to see how treating citizens of India in the same way as those of the USA would have this effect, and the 1968 Act clearly lays down that there is free entry to the UK for anyone holding a 'UK and colonies' passport who is ordinarily resident in the UK. But the opportunity could well be taken, when revising the law, to clarify what constitutes British citizenship. It is normally accepted that a citizen of a country is entitled to enter it. However, the 1968 Act has split holders of passports marked 'citizen of the UK and colonies' into two categories: on the one hand, those normally resident in the UK, or who were born in the UK, or one of whose parents or paternal grandparents

---

1 E.g., R. B. Davison, *Commonwealth Immigrants,* Institute of Race Relations, 1964.

2 Peter Evans, 'The Cruel Deception', *The Times,* 1 November, 1969.

was born in the UK; on the other hand, the remainder. The first group is entitled to free entry, the second is not.

Since the same passport now covers two distinct categories, it might be better to recognise this distinction more formally—one passport for UK citizens and one for citizens of the colonies. All persons normally resident in the UK would be eligible for UK citizenship, which would entitle them to come and go at will. A classification of status on these lines could only make existing immigrants feel more secure. This, of course, implies that the existing immigrants should be accepted and integrated into the community. Even if one believes that the original immigration policy was misguided, it is hard to see that there is now any alternative to accepting the immigrants and working for integration.

Finally, something should be done to help the unfortunate Asians of East Africa, who chose UK citizenship as an insurance policy against racial persecution, but found that the company refused to pay up when they made a claim. The UK's debt to them may now have to be paid in cash, to assist their re-settlement in India. If there is a limit on foreign exchange expenditure, the money could come out of aid to the countries which are expelling them.

What is now needed is a candid discussion of the existing law, and the preparation of a better one. We must try to avoid stop-gap, piecemeal legislation like the 1962 and 1968 Acts. On these current problems of immigration and citizenship, some words of Lord Keynes seem as appropriate as they were to the problems of socialism and capitalism in the inter-war period.

> 'We need by an effort of the mind to elucidate our own feelings. At present our sympathy and our judgements are liable to be on different sides, which is a painful and paralysing state of mind. In the field of action, reformers will not be successful until they can steadily pursue a clear and definite object with their intellects and their feelings in tune.'[1]

---

[1] 'The End of Laisser-faire', in *Essays in Persuasion*, Macmillan, 1931 (reprinted 1952).

FURTHER READING

In addition to the books and articles referred to in the text, the following may be mentioned:

Davison, R. B., *Black British,* Institute of Race Relations, London, 1966.

Jackson, John Archer, *The Irish in Britain,* London, 1963.

Manley, Douglas, *et al, The West Indian Comes to England,* Family Welfare Association, London, 1960.

Rashmi, Desui, *Indian Immigrants in Britain,* Oxford University Press, 1963.

Davison, R. B., *Commonwealth Immigrants,* Institute of Race Relations, 1964.

Bouscaran, A. T., *International Migration Since 1945,* Praeger, New York, 1963.

UNESCO, *The Positive Contribution of Immigrants,* 1955.

Kulischer, E. M., *Europe on the Move: War and Population Changes,* New York, 1948.

Burney, E., *Housing on Trial: A study of Immigrants and Local Government,* Institute of Race Relations, 1967.

Banton, M., *Race Relations,* Tavistock Publications, 1967.

Wright, P. L., *The Coloured Worker in British Industry,* Oxford University Press for the Institute of Race Relations, 1968.